GREECE TRAVEL GUIDE

UNLOCK THE COMPLETE AND UP-TO-DATE PASSPORT TO DISCOVER HIDDEN TREASURES, MYTH, MAGIC, AND MEDITERRANEAN BEAUTY OF GREECE

By

JARMAN CORBIN

Greece Travel Guide 2024

Unlock the Complete and Up-to-Date Passport to Discover Hidden Treasures, Myth, Magic, and Mediterranean Beauty of Greece

© Copyright 2024

All rights reserved.

This document's objective is to provide accurate and dependable information about the subject and issue at hand. The publisher sells the book with the knowledge that it is not bound to provide accounting, legally permissible, or otherwise qualifying services. If legal or professional assistance is required, it is prudent to consult a knowledgeable specialist.

From a Declaration of Principles that an American Bar Association Committee and a Publishers and Associations Committee jointly recognized and approved.

No portion of this publication, whether electronic or printed, may be reproduced, duplicated, or transmitted in any form or by any means. It is highly illegal to record this publication, and storage of this document is permitted only with the publisher's prior consent.

The trademarks are utilized without the permission or backing of the trademark owner, and the trademark is published without the consent or backing of the trademark owner. All trademarks and registered trademarks referenced in this book are the property of their respective owners and are not associated with this publication.

Contents

INTRODUCTION 1
    DEVELOPMENT OF TOURISM 3
    WHY GREECE? 3

TRAVEL PLANNING 5
    HOW TO TRAVEL THERE 5
    WHEN TO GO 6
    WHAT TO PACK 7
        Personal Item for Greece 8
        Packing Electronics for Greece 8
        Pack Clothes for Greece 8
        Packing Tips 9
        What to Pack for Greece: Spring and Summer 10

BUDGETING YOUR TRIP 12
        How much are Greece package excursions going to cost? 12
        Independent Travel 13
        Budget Tips for Greece 14

ITINERARY PLANNING 17
    10 DAY GREECE ITINERARY 18
    LINKING DESTINATIONS 18
        Best for history buffs: Athens 18
        Santorini is best for glamour 19
        Corfu best for families 19
        Crete best for foodies: 19
        Kefalonia is best for solos 20
        The Peloponnese is best for off-the-beaten-track 20
        Thessaloniki 21
    BUILDING YOUR ITINERARY 21
        Planning Your Greek Island Itinerary 21
        Useful Advice for Traveling to Greek Islands 22

TRANSPORTATION TIPS: GETTING FROM PLACE TO PLACE 24
    BY BUS 25
    VIA TRAIN 25

- BY SEA 26
- FERRIES 27
- BY PLANE 28
- BY CAR, MOTORCYCLE AND TAXI 29

GREECE TOP EXPERIENCES 34

MUST-SEE FAVORITES PLACES 34
- *Discover the Acropolis, Acropolis Museum and Sounio Temple* 35
- *Wine Tasting on Santorini* 35
- *Santorini Sunset Catamaran Cruise* 35
- *Crete Wine and Music Tasting Tour* 35
- *Sail Around Beautiful Milos* 35
- *Tour Knossos on Crete to Discover the Palace Myths* 36
- *Sea Kayaking on Santorini* 36
- *Discover the World of Naxian Marble* 36
- *Mountainous Apeiranthos* 36
- *Take a Santorini cooking class.* 36
- *Become a Mykonian for a Day.* 37
- *Little Venice at Sunset with Delos and Rhenia Island in the background.* 37
- *An All-Day Trip from Athens to Hydra.* 37
- *A Whole Day Wine Tour of Nafplio and Nemea.* 38
- *A Photo Tour of Magnificent Meteora.* 38
- *Minoan Food and Art on Crete.* 38
- *Go on a day trip to Athens and discover Ancient Delphi.* 38
- *Sail to the Small Cyclades and Rina Cave by going around Naxos.* 38

TOP SIGHTS AND HIDDEN GEMS 39
- *Kastellorizo* 39
- *Ithaca* 40
- *Milos* 41
- *Paxi* 41
- *Chios* 42
- *Mani* 42
- *Epirus* 43
- *Monemvasia* 43
- *Skopelos* 44
- *Amorgos* 45
- *Meteora* 45

LOCAL CULTURE AND CUSTOMS 47
TRADITIONAL FESTIVITIES 48
Name day celebration 48
May Day 48
Engagement 48
Carnival 48
Clean Monday 49
Easter 49
Greek Independence Day 49
The Ohi Day 49
Superstitions 50

SPECIAL EXPERIENCES 52
SELF-GUIDED WALKING TOURS 52
Crete Self-Guided Hike 53
Zagoria Secret Villages Walking Tour 53
Santorini and Naxos on Foot Self-Guided Walking Tour 53
Andros Trail Self-Guided Walk 54
Mount Olympus Guided Walk 54
Ancient Greece on Foot Holiday 54
Crete Mountains and Coast Guided Walk 55

EXPLORING BARS AND LOCAL LIQUEURS 56
DRINKING IN GREECE 56
A communal activity of the Greeks 56
Greek liqueurs and meze to the rescue 56
Greek cocktails 57
Greek wine 58

AVOIDING TOURIST TRAPS 60
Exploring the Most Well-liked Islands 60
Dining on the Beach 60
Traveling Around by Tour Bus 61
Purchasing Expensive Souvenirs 61
Utilizing Social Media to Visit Restaurants 61
Purchasing Rooftop Views from a Chain Hotel 62
Purchasing Fake Designer Items 62
Taking Sunset Photos on Santorini 62

 Visiting a Resort That Is All-Inclusive *63*
 Not Verifying Prices at a Restaurant Before Eating *63*
 Going to the Big Attractions at Midday *63*
 The taxi trap *64*

ACCOMMODATIONS AND DINING 65
BEST CULINARY EXPERIENCES IN GREECE'S TOP HOTEL RESTAURANTS 65
 Mavro Restaurant at Kivotos Santorini *66*
 Botrini Mykonos *66*
 Matsuhisa in Paros *66*
 *Galazia Hytra Restaurant, Summer Senses * Paros* *67*
 The Coast by Tamarisk at Numo in Crete *67*
 Pere Ubu at Kalesma Mykonos *67*
 Barbouni Restaurant at Costa Navarino *68*
 Olvo at MINOIS Hotel in Paros *68*
 Milos at Xenodocheio Milos in Athens *68*
 Santa Marina, a Luxury Collection Resort, Mykonos *68*

USEFUL PHRASES AND WORDS TO LEARN 69
BASIC GREEK WORDS AND PHRASES 69

CONCLUSION 72

INTRODUCTION

G reece is a country with an archipelago of around 2,000 islands that is situated in Southern Europe near the southern tip of the Balkan Peninsula. Greece shares land boundaries with the Mediterranean Sea, the Aegean Sea, the Ionian Sea, Bulgaria, and Albania. Greece is ideally situated to dominate both the southern approach to the Turkish Straits and the Aegean Sea. The president serves as the head of state and the prime minister as the head of government of the parliamentary republic. Greece is a market economy with free market principles dictating how much goods and services cost. Greece is a part of the EU, or European Union.

Greece still receives 90% of its high season visitors from within Europe, but it is quickly rising to prominence among global travelers.

Its main draws are well-known across the world for their connections to the Minoan, Mycenaean, and Ancient Greek eras, which were captured in the compositions of eminent poets, dramatists, and philosophers about 2,000 years ago. Travelers' all-time favorites are exploring the wonders of Athens, Mycenae in the Peloponnese, and Knossos on Crete. But Greece is more than just historical ruins; contemporary attractions like fantastic beaches, exciting water sports, outdoor activities, and tavernas by the water all have a place in the ideal Greek vacation.

With their open arms and hearts, the Greek people extend their famous hospitality to everyone, making them one of the most hospitable, kind, and helpful people on the planet. You'll quickly become a part of the community whether you're lodging in a five-star resort or a locally owned coastal bed and breakfast with a few rooms available for rent. Both dining out and lodging offer good value for the money.

Numerous options are available for both mainland Greece and the Greek islands, accommodating a wide range of vacation preferences, from history enthusiasts to beachcombers. The majority of historic sites are concentrated in the close vicinity of a significant town center, and ferry boats from mainland ports make it simple to travel between the islands.

The Sanctuary of Asclepios and the 3,000-year-old Mycenae and Tiryns are easily accessible by car, while Delphi and Olympia may be reached in a single day from Athens. Situated on towering cliffs, the ancient Mount Athos and its crow's-nest monasteries are located in the northern region of the country on the Chalkidiki peninsula.

There are limited rail services in Greece, thus the best ways to see its various sights are by car or ferry. Since the local bus only stops at the closest village, which is a lengthy, sweltering walk from the landmarks, renting a car allows guests the freedom to drive to remote spots. Driving isn't too difficult, besides the winding mountain roads; but, in rural regions, domestic animals like goats and donkeys could think the roads are their own! Except in isolated rural areas, bus travel is reasonably priced, pleasant, and air-conditioned. Ferries make for convenient, picturesque travel between Piraeus and all of the principal islands.

Greece is a must-visit country! This stunning nation is distinguished by its hilly terrain, amazing weather, several alluring islands, lengthy sandy beaches, countless attractions of all types, and much more!

Check out our travel guides to discover the ideal spots to organize your vacations in one or more of the well-known vacation spots!

Development Of Tourism

The "LONDON Hotel" was the first hotel in Greece, and it was built in Nafplio, the country's initial capital, in 1834. After the infamous "GRANDE BRETAGNE" in Syntagma Square opened its doors for business in 1878, Greece's hospitality industry began to progressively expand.

In the late 1960s and especially in the early 1970s, Greek tourism began to take off.

Greece has steadily grown over the years to rank among the most popular travel destinations for Americans, Europeans, and Asians.

Since three-quarters of travelers prefer to visit Greece during this time of year, May through September is considered the peak travel season in Greece.

People from all over the world are drawn to Greece by its sunny weather, warm beaches, and diverse landscapes, which offer Greek hospitality and a tranquil way of life.

The Greek economy heavily depends on tourist earnings; in fact, many refer to it as the nation's heavy industry.

Numerous hotels, restaurants, cafes, gift stores, and other businesses have been established in each location, resulting in the creation of numerous jobs and ongoing support for enterprises.

In addition to summer vacations, efforts are being made to promote various types of travel: in addition to winter vacations, therapeutic spas, ecotourism, working vacations, and discovery vacations are starting to gain popularity.

Additionally, island hopping itineraries and island cruises are growing in popularity.

Why Greece?

Greece is a well-known nation, well-known for its spotless beaches and extensive history.

The past of the nation is magnificently depicted at hundreds of archeological and historical monuments; also, there's a reason Athens is known as an open-air museum!

The Greek mainland is primarily covered in mountains, with certain valleys having extremely fruitful ground.

Greece is encircled by water as well, specifically the Aegean and Ionian Seas.

There are about 6000 islands and islets in the nation, but only 227 of them are populated. These are the most well-liked Greek travel locations, particularly during the summer. Whether they are large or little, lush or dry, perfect for adventurous or leisurely getaways, they have the amenities and necessities to provide you with safe and enjoyable travels!

Several well-known island getaways are:

Mykonos, with its international vibe.

The world's most romantic sunset can be found in Santorini.

The island of knights, Rhodes, with its fairytale castles and butterflies.

Crete, with its spirit of revolt.

Ios, with its exuberant evenings.

Corfu, in a Venetian fashion.

The home of Odysseus is Ithaca.

The greenest Greek island is Samos.

Skiathos, has lengthy, fine-sand beaches.

These are but a handful of the most well-known Greek paradises.

Numerous of them have airports and are conveniently reachable by flight from Athens or other European cities directly. You may also go to all of them via ferry.

TRAVEL PLANNING

Step foot in the magnificent nation of historic heroes and gorgeous scenery. Greece has always been a popular travel destination because of its enthralling myths and stories, breathtaking islands, and Aegean Sea. Greece is therefore the ideal travel location for everyone. A trip to Greece is always an excellent choice, regardless of whether you are a romantic pair or a fantastic lone traveler.

In summary, flying is the most convenient method of visiting Greece. The most well-known international airports are found in Heraklion, Santorini, Mykonos, Athens, and Thessaloniki.

You can take domestic aircraft, ferries, buses, or trains to go around.

HOW TO TRAVEL THERE

You shouldn't be concerned about traveling to Greece because it's a fairly accessible location. There are several ways to get there:

Airplane.

By plane is the quickest and most convenient method to get there, particularly if you reside in the US or Europe.

Regular flights from a wide range of international airlines arrive in Athens, and during the summer months, there are plenty of direct flights to several islands in Greece (including Santorini, Mykonos, and others) that are served by international airports.

There are some regions with a national airport that only handles flights from Athens.

Taking a ferry from the ports of Piraeus, Rafina, and Lavrio in Athens is an alternate (and less expensive) way to get to your destination.

Finding the nearest international airport is the greatest option for getting to a Greek island without an airport. For instance, those wishing to visit the island of Amorgos can arrive at Santorini's international airport and take a ferry from Santorini to Amorgos.

Ferry.

All year round, there are ferry services between Greece and Italy. More specifically, travelers from Europe who wish to bring a car or campervan can do so with ease thanks to the ferries that run between Patra, Igoumenitsa, and Corfu in Greece and Venice, Ancona, Bari, and Brindisi in Italy.

Greeka or FerriesinGreece are the places where you may purchase ferry tickets.

When to Go

Officially, April through October is the tourist season; July and August are the two peak months.

During these two hot months, most people visit the popular islands, while the more remote ones maintain their tranquil atmosphere.

The months of April through June are ideal if you're searching for seclusion, leisure, and less crowds. It will be simpler to locate inexpensive lodging and get less expensive flight tickets during this time of year.

While most people associate Greece with summer tourism, the mainland is also a fantastic place to visit for winter city breaks and ski vacations.

Off-season in Athens is so much fun because there are fewer tourists at the ancient monuments and it's not as hot outside!

While numerous more ski areas are located in the country's north, Arachova and Kalavryta are the most well-known. The time of year you visit Greece will have a significant impact on your trip. Summer is the best season for activities, fun with the family, and swimming in the Mediterranean, but because everything is so busy, booking is essential and rates are at their highest.

Spring and fall are the best times to visit because things are less expensive and there are more accommodations and resources accessible. Winter travel is a somber, affordable escape that's perfect for walking, trekking, and quiet excursions where you'll frequently be the only guests. Remember that during the off-season, some establishments will close entirely.

What to Pack

There are certain things you never want to forget when embarking on an extraordinary journey. You will require identification, travel documents, and prescription drugs.

Whatever else you bring, don't forget to include:

Wallet: With ID, passport, cash and cards.

Travel Documents: including, if necessary, travel insurance and visa documentation.

.**Medications**: Carry extras, copies of prescriptions, and generic names of medications for everyday, essential, and allergy needs.

In case of loss, make a duplicate copy of your credit card information and the front page of your passport.

Prescriptions, insurance documents, and vital papers should all be kept in two locations at minimum: on your phone and in the cloud. For backup, paper copies are excellent, but keep the copies somewhere different from the originals.

Personal Item for Greece.

Pack a personal item whether you're traveling by air, land, or water to Greece. If you're going to the beach or sightseeing, you should have a daypack that can hold your essentials close at hand.

An excellent option is a packable bag, such as the Outbreaker Daypack, which you can tuck away in your carry-on luggage when not in use.

After making sure you have everything you need, use the Personal Item Packing List and add the following for Greece:

- Sunscreen, bug spray, and mosquito anti-itch ointment (travel sized)
- Sunglasses

Packing Electronics for Greece

Ideally, you won't have to spend time on your computer and can instead take in Greece's natural beauty and history.

- Laptop and charger (if needed)
- Tablet and charger
- Smartphone, headphones, and charger
- Kindle and charger
- Camera, memory cards, connecting cables, and charger (if needed)
- External battery

Pack Clothes for Greece

Greece exudes a carefree and relaxed air. Try to combine low-key elegance with functionality, portability, lightweight design, and ease of use. During your stay in Greece, you should expect to travel from the country to the sea and from city to country. Recall that your buddies are the layers. It's vital to wear sturdy walking shoes or sandals.

A scarf, a light jacket, and sunglasses can make any ensemble look put together.

What to carry for Greece is as follows:

- 3-5 pairs of socks
- 4-7 pairs underwear
- 2 bras
- 3 short sleeve t-shirts or tank tops
- 1 long sleeve shirt
- 1-2 skirts or sun dresses
- 1-2 pairs of casual pants, shorts, capris, leggings or skirts
- 1 pair jeans
- 1 pair flip-flops
- 1 pair comfortable non-slip walking shoes
- 1 pair nicer shoes for evenings out
- 1 pair pajamas or athleisure clothes that do double duty
- 1 set workout or hiking gear
- 1 lightweight sweater or jacket
- 1 swimsuit

PACKING TIPS

Men must wear jackets to many of the hotels, restaurants, and cruise ship casinos at night, while women must wear slightly more formal attire, including shoes with straps. When packing, think about the tasks you'll be performing.

Consider wearing water shoes if you're going to the beaches or islands to protect your toes from coral and rough, slick patches in the water.

Steer clear of "travel apparel" and t-shirts with culturally relevant slogans or symbols that scream "tourist" to blend in. Bring at least knee-length pants and a scarf for your shoulders if you're visiting places of worship or culture.

What to Pack for Greece: Spring and Summer

While Greece's cities, countrysides, and island getaways are always open, summertime is when most visitors arrive. When the sun shines brightly, the waters are warm, the skies are blue, and most people are willing to brave the throng and wait in line to be there.

If you want to escape the peak chaos, think about visiting your Mediterranean resort in the shoulder season, which runs from mid-April to early-June, or even later in September when the advent of autumnal air cools the weather.

Verify the precise areas you will be visiting. Cities and coastal areas will experience different temperatures.

What to Bring for a Spring Trip to Greece

Greece's spring season lasts from March to early May. The range of temperatures is 55–65 degrees Fahrenheit. There could be mild rainstorms and colder weather.

For Greece's springtime, add:

- Rain jacket
- Travel umbrella
- Close-toed shoes
- Scarf for cool days

WHAT TO BRING FOR A SUMMER TRIP TO GREECE

Greece experiences its summer from the end of May to the end of August. You should anticipate 75–90 degree Fahrenheit temps. While inland regions can experience extreme humidity and temperatures well over 100 degrees Fahrenheit, islands can have dry heat and cooler evening breezes.

To Greece's summertime add:

- Water bottle.
- Wide-brimmed hat.
- Sunscreen and bug spray.
- Extra swimsuit.
- Lightweight layer.
- One extra pair of shoes or flip flops.

BUDGETING YOUR TRIP

Greece is one of the most sought-after travel destinations in the world. It is home to breathtaking islands, a rich and varied culinary legacy, ancient monasteries, a raucous party scene, and a history spanning thousands of years.

But the majority of people don't consider it to be inexpensive. When one mentions Greece, most people immediately think of Santorini's white and blue cliffside houses, boutique hotels, elegant dining, exciting nightlife, and island-hopping cruises. Everything that says, "This trip won't be inexpensive!"

What is the cost of traveling to Greece for one, two, or three weeks?

Typically, a one-person trip to Greece costs approximately $1,374 (€1,278), while a two-person vacation typically costs $2,748 (€2,555). This covers lodging, meals, local transit, and sightseeing.

The average cost of a two-week trip to Greece is approximately $2,748 (€2,555) for an individual and $5,497 (€5,110) for a couple. This price covers lodging, meals, local transit, and touring.

Note that pricing can change depending on your speed, manner of travel, and other factors. When traveling as a family of three or four, the cost per person generally decreases because shared hotel accommodations and lower tickets for children are available. Over an extended duration of slower travel, your daily budget will decrease as well. A couple spending a month in Greece together will often have a daily budget that is less than that of a single individual visiting for a week.

An average one-person vacation to Greece costs $5,890 (€5,475), while a two-person trip costs $11,779 (€10,950). The daily cost will rise as you visit more locations because transportation expenses will rise.

How much are Greece package excursions going to cost?

Though they are typically more expensive than solo travel, organized tours provide convenience and the assurance that your vacation has been expertly designed by a travel specialist.

In Greece, the average daily cost of an organized tour package is $244. Although the total cost, duration, number of stops, and quality of each tour vary, this is the average daily cost based on our research of the available guided tours.

INDEPENDENT TRAVEL

Independent travel offers numerous advantages, such as cost-effectiveness, liberty, adaptability, and the chance to dictate your own adventures.

Based on the experiences of other independent travelers, all of the travel expenses listed below.

Is traveling to Greece expensive?

Greece is a reasonably cost travel destination. In terms of travel expenses, it is comparable to most other nations. Transportation, lodging, and food costs are all fairly affordable.

Greece is reasonably priced in comparison to other European nations, despite the continent's reputation as an expensive place to live. Travel expenses here are similar to those in Denmark or Luxembourg.

Greece's Average Prices

When visiting Greece, you can anticipate the following, on average (prices are in EUR):

- Hostel dorm: 15-25/night.

- Hostel private room: 30-60/night (though, on Santorini or Mykonos, expect as a high as 75).

- Seafood dinner: 15-20.

- Lunch specials: 10-12.

- Cocktails: 12-15.

- Bottled water at the grocery store: 0.50.

- Bottled water (in a restaurant): 1.

- Major museums/historic sites: 10-20.

- Beer: 3-4.

- Land tours: 15-50.

- Boat tours: 10-35.

- Greek salad: 5.50–8.

- Greek main dish: 8-12.

- Public intracity buses/subways: 1-2/ride.

- Wine/food tours: 100-125 (40 for a half-day).

- Ferries: 25-70/ride.

- Budget hotel: 40-60/night (though, you can sometimes find guesthouses for as low as 25).

- Gyro (and other cheap to-go food): 2.50-3.50.

- Glass of wine at a restaurant: 2.5–4.

Budget Tips for Greece

Greece is surprisingly affordable. Greek meals, wine glasses, hostel dorms, and public transportation are reasonably priced. You can find some fairly great lodging for 30 to 50 euros per night. In Greece, there are numerous methods to cut costs without compromising comfort. Here's how to do it:

Apply the Bread/Greek Salad Rule.

My top rule is this one! Is a restaurant pricey or cheap? Here's a sensible generalization: The restaurant is affordable if the bread cover costs less than .50 EUR or if a Greek salad costs less than 7 EUR. The prices are average if the cover costs about 1 EUR and a salad costs 7-8.50 EUR. Any more than that, and the location gets pricey.

Eat super cheap.

Most street delicacies, including gyros, only cost a few €. They may keep you filled for less than 10 EUR a day and are quick and simple!

Take out a scooter rental.

Rent a moped if you plan to stay somewhere (perhaps on one of the islands) for an extended period of time. It is more handy than the bus and less expensive than a car. It's the ideal way to venture off the main road and a fun way to visit the many villages and cities.

Avert the beaten route.

Greece has the lowest prices once you leave the well-traveled areas. Travel to less-frequented locations to find price reductions of up to 30%!

Make an overnight ferry reservation.

The cost of Greece's ferries might increase significantly if you want to visit several islands. You can save up to half of the usual cost by using the overnight ferries, which also spare you from having to stay an extra night.

Possess an ISIC card.

Make sure you have a valid student card in order to receive discounted admission to museums and other tourist attractions. Most places that do not accept a foreign student ID also do not accept the ISIC.

Couchsurfing.

A great way to meet people in the area and score a free place to stay is through couchsurfing.

Purchase wine from the store.

A fantastic bottle of wine may be purchased in supermarkets for as low as 4 EUR. Drink in advance to save money; it's far less expensive than going out to bars.

Obtain a ferry pass.

There are 4- and 6-trip ferry pass options available from Eurail/Interrail. The sole restriction is that the ferries you can take are only Blue Star and Hellenic Seaways. These boats are usually slower and larger, and depending on the islands, you may have to make a connection elsewhere. To determine whether the pass is worthwhile, you'll need to do some preliminary route investigation. To find out if it works for you, I would look up routes on FerryHopper.

Use the bus or train.

Although they occasionally operate on odd timetables, buses are the most convenient means of transportation in Greece. There, taxi fares are exceedingly high, so try to avoid using them as much as possible.

OBTAIN BUNDLED TICKETS.

In Greece, the majority of historical sites have prices that make purchasing a combination ticket a better value. Purchase it if the websites you plan to offer that. You'll save money by doing this.

WHEN POSSIBLE, USE POINTS.

It will be preferable to utilize your accrued points and miles—which can be exchanged for cash—to make hotel reservations when staying at less expensive establishments (anything under $100 USD). You can make significant financial savings with just a few thousand points per night. Here is more information about getting started.

HIRE A VEHICLE.

In Greece, renting a car can be quite affordable. When made in advance, rates as low as 15 EUR per day are offered. Drivers must be at least 21 years old and have held a license for a year. Additionally necessary is an international driving permit. Use Discover Cars to get the greatest deals on rental cars.

Like any other nation, Greece offers a variety of affordable solutions. It's true that you may spend a fortune there—many visitors opt for a posh, pricey escape. However, going there doesn't have to cost the earth. You may enjoy a fantastic trip and stay inside your budget by implementing the above advice.

ITINERARY PLANNING

Understanding the value of a carefully thought-out schedule is crucial while visiting Greece, a nation renowned for its natural beauty and rich history. Greece is a cultural melting pot of ancient traditions, breathtaking scenery, and deeply ingrained customs. Every location has something unique to offer, from the calm beaches of several islands to the ancient streets of Athens. Greece is a remarkable destination that offers a comprehensive introduction to its distinctive features and cultural attractions through a personalized itinerary.

A well-planned itinerary ensures a seamless and fulfilling vacation, regardless of your interests—uncovering the lesser-known natural beauties of the mainland and the islands, relishing the vibrant local cuisine, or learning about the mysteries of historic places.

Together, let's design a tour that suits your tastes, style, and speed to make sure your time in Greece is genuinely unforgettable.

10 day Greece itinerary

Get ready for an amazing 10-day Greek vacation where you will be able to take in a wonderful blend of natural wonders and cultural sites.

Start your adventure in Athens, where on the first day you will witness the magnificence of the Acropolis. We'll start Day 2 with a walk around Plaka's historic streets and neoclassical buildings. You'll go to Delphi on day three to see the stunning mountain scenery and learn about ancient oracles.

You'll visit the quaint seaside village of Nafplio on day four, where you'll find historical treasures. Travel to Crete and spend a day in Knossos immersing yourself in Minoan history on day 5. You'll go to the ancient attractions and local marketplaces of Rhodes, a medieval city, on the sixth day of your trip.

You'll spend days seven and eight on the picturesque island of Santorini, which is renowned for its stunning surroundings. Discover the historic site of Akrotiri and lose yourself in the distinct beauty of the island. Explore Corfu's ancient tapestry on day nine, which was influenced by Venetian, French, and British architecture.

On day 10, come to an end to your journey by going back to Athens for a final exploration or sleep. With a focus on natural wonders and different riches of Greek culture, this 10-day itinerary unveils a new aspect of Greece's rich past every day.

Linking destinations

Best for history buffs: Athens

Greece's elegant capital is a must-see city vacation that is enjoyable throughout the year. From May to October, ships depart from the port of Piraeus, making it simple to take a beach or nature holiday.

Since the most of the ancient Greek sites are concentrated on and around the Acropolis Hill, you should base yourself in central Monastiraki and Plaka for quick trips so you can start seeing things right away. If you have a little more time to spare, you might opt to stay in the more laid-back Psyrri or Pangrati, where concept boutiques and pavement cafes coexist with tucked-away eateries and craft beer bars. Or Kolonaki, the chic "Knightsbridge of Athens," home to the most opulent lodgings.

SANTORINI IS BEST FOR GLAMOUR.

This Cycladic icon is no secret; ever since Instagram and the jet-set discovered it, this island has become known as the place where a thousand selfies were taken. However, upon visiting, it becomes evident why: the island's western (caldera) side plunges into the sea in a picturesque manner, forming the partially submerged edge of a long-dormant volcano rim. Scattered over its summits are uniformly gorgeous residences and hotels in the Cycladic style, many with ribbons of hot pink bougainvillea and lit plunge pools. You'll have the feeling of being the star of a movie if you hang around Oia and Imerovigli and go on a sunset yacht sail around the coast.

There are more reasonably priced accommodations on the island close to charming hilltop villages and flatter, black volcanic beaches, but if you're only visiting Santorini for its distinctive appearance, you should stay along the caldera shore. Because there are millions of steps linking the structures and sheer dropoffs, it's not a family-friendly place. Furthermore, everything in this area is more expensive than it is in other parts of Greece, including hotel rooms, meals, and drinks. least expensive option? Not in a manner. Worth the money? Indeed.

CORFU BEST FOR FAMILIES

The key word here is "ease": young families will adore Corfu's sensible tourism sector, in addition to having the shortest travel time from the UK. Arrive at its east coast airport, which is serviced by plenty of taxis and has a well-paved coast road connecting it to hotels. The majority of resorts are within a 30-minute drive away, although more remote villas and less well-known hotels may be found a little further north and northeast of the city. Try the Marbella, Ikos, or Grecotel groups for a few of the most well-known hotels that successfully combine style and family friendliness, and there are plenty more that are just warm and reasonably priced. A selection of items designated for adults are popular among couples. This large, forested island is ideal for renting a car and exploring, even though the tourism sector is easily accessible and well-established. Take a ferry to Paxos island from the sand-fringed north and west coast's charming old port, Corfu Town.

CRETE BEST FOR FOODIES:

There is a lot more to discover even if you have just visited one beach town or area because this island is so large that a nonstop drive across it would take about five hours. Outstanding cuisine, however, is something you can get everywhere in Crete because of the region's long farming history and strong emphasis on product, seasonality, and origin. It also produces a lot of olive oil and has its own varieties of salads and cheeses from the area. The trendiest eateries in other parts of Greece are frequently influenced by Cretan food.

There are two airports on the north coast where you can land: Chania to the west and Heraklion to the east. Since they are more than two hours apart, be sure to reserve the best lodging possible. A large island like this offers a wealth of options and diversity: family-friendly, reasonably priced beach villages, chic port cities, historic archeological sites, and secluded coves that can only be accessed by boat are all there. The cost in kind? a good deal of planning and investigation.

Kefalonia is best for solos

While Crete has a bus network that is unusual for Greece and is also ideal for single travelers and backpackers, Kefalonia boasts some of the most varied landscapes, complete with historic cities, breathtaking beaches, and an enormous selection of lodging options. This large Ionian island also offers a couple of bus routes that, for a few euros, let you leave for charming little coastal villages like Assos, Fiskardo, and Poros, all of which have boats that take you to smaller islands. The sophisticated port of Argostoli is located close to the airport. Ferries from as cheap as £10 or £15 each way can take you to adjacent islands like Lefkada and Ithaca.

This system of reasonably priced flats, unique locations, and transportation choices is ideal for being impulsive and exploring new areas. It's also one of the most picturesque islands in Greece, with pastel-colored homes, cliffs that drop off to reveal mountain goats, glittering sea caves, and pristine beaches. To gain a sense of the past, bring a copy of Captain Corelli's Mandolin, which is set here.

The Peloponnese is best for off-the-beaten-track

This overlooked portion of the mainland has been seeing a trickle of tourists for decades, but it has only lately been noticeable on the major travel scene. Located southwest of Athens, this oblong-shaped peninsula boasts pine-scented mountains, dilapidated monasteries, secluded settlements, and gorgeous sandy beaches, particularly in the center Mani Peninsula and Cape Malea.

You'll need a car to explore this rough area, which boasts sights like the Unesco-listed Epidaurus amphitheater, the archeological site of Mycenae, the honeycomb-colored castle of Monemvasia, and Mystras, a 13th-century Byzantine city near the famous warrior state of Sparta. Along the way, there are charming seaside towns and secluded spa resorts to visit.

THESSALONIKI

Thessaloniki, in Macedonia, is the second-biggest city in Greece, if Athens is the most well-known and its capital. Among the many well-known landmarks here are Mount Olympus, the Church of Agia Sofia, and the White Tower of Thessaloniki, making a visit essential.

Thessaloniki is the capital of Macedonia and the cultural hub of Northern Greece. It is a modern city with a bustling commercial district, colorful food markets, skyscrapers, vibrant festivals, social events, and a buzzing nightlife. Moreover, it has a rich history with famous Byzantine walls, museums, and art galleries.

Every visitor to Greece will have the chance to see the timeless beauty of ancient architectural marvels combined with the poetic beauty of the natural world. Greece, the gorgeous nation steeped in mythology, is without a doubt the most breathtaking destination for travelers from all over the world.

BUILDING YOUR ITINERARY

Greek island hopping is a distinctive and adaptable approach to experience the many landscapes and cultures of the nation. Every island has a unique charm and personality, from the sophisticated vibes of Mykonos to the serene beauty of Naxos and the fascination of Santorini's volcanic landscape.

You may customize your itinerary to fit your interests when island hopping, whether you're looking for exciting nightlife, sun-drenched beaches, or ancient wonders. Long-distance travel might be a headache, but with short boat rides between islands, you can visit multiple sites with ease.

PLANNING YOUR GREEK ISLAND ITINERARY

A seamless and enjoyable travel may be ensured by taking into account a few important elements while organizing your Greek island hopping adventure:

SELECT THE ISLANDS THAT YOU WANT.

Choosing the right islands for your schedule can be difficult with over 200 inhabited islands to consider.

Determine your top priorities first, be they historical places, immaculate beaches, or true Greek culture. The Dodecanese, Ionian Islands, and Cyclades are popular island groups for island hopping.

THINK ABOUT TRAVEL ARRANGEMENTS.

Although most Greek islands are connected by ferry, it's important to plan ahead and check ferry schedules and routes in order to maximize your trip time. Arrange your schedule to avoid lengthy boat rides and to give yourself enough time to see each place.

MAKE ROOM FOR ADAPTABILITY.

Even while it could be tempting to include as many islands as you can in your itinerary, it's important to leave time for flexibility and relaxation. It may be quite taxing to bounce from island to island, so plan rest days to unwind and recuperate.

MAKE RESERVATIONS FOR LODGING IN ADVANCE.

Popular islands might see a rapid fill-up of accommodations, particularly during the summer months.

Make your hotel reservations well in advance to minimize disappointment, particularly if you have certain tastes or financial restrictions.

USEFUL ADVICE FOR TRAVELING TO GREEK ISLANDS.

Take into consideration the following helpful advice to get the most out of your Greek island-hopping trip:

Pack Light: When island hopping, packing light is crucial because there are a lot of ferry rides and little room for storage. Remain with basics like sunblock, light-colored clothing, and cozy walking shoes.

Remain Hydrated: Throughout your trip, remember to stay hydrated due to the strong Mediterranean sun. Bring a reusable water bottle with you and make use of the numerous springs and fountains the islands have to offer.

Accept Local cuisine: With its abundance of tasty meats, crisp salads, and fresh seafood, Greek gastronomy is a highlight of every island hopping excursion. Don't pass up the opportunity to try regional delicacies like souvlaki, moussaka, and fresh Greek salads.

Respect Local Customs: Greece is renowned for its kind hospitality, but it's important to be mindful of regional traditions and customs. When visiting places of worship, dress modestly, say "kalimera" (good morning) to the locals, and pick up a few simple Greek phrases to express your respect for the way of life.

Take your time: There's more to island hopping than just crossing places off a list. Enjoy a leisurely supper by the sea, watch the sunset from a cliffside taverna, or just unwind on a quiet beach as you immerse yourself in the beauty and rhythm of island life.

Your Greek Island Adventure Awaits.

Greek island hopping is an incredible experience that guarantees romance, excitement, and lifelong memories. You can expect an exciting and adventurous Greek island itinerary, whether you choose to explore the famous landmarks of Santorini, party all night in Mykonos, or find the hidden jewels of Naxos and Paros.

So gather your belongings, set out on your island-hopping journey, and be ready to be mesmerized by the allure and splendor of the Greek islands. Are you ready to explore? Your ideal Greece itinerary is waiting for you.

TRANSPORTATION TIPS: GETTING FROM PLACE TO PLACE

Greece has a variety of transportation choices, so it's helpful to know how much they'll cost and how simple it will be to get from one area to another. Greece's islands, for instance, are primarily connected via ferry. While renting a car is still a common choice, it's important to understand your alternatives for public transit, particularly if your vacation entails traveling to or through the Greek Islands.

In Greece, buses are the primary mode of overland public transportation. There are few train networks, made much more so by the most recent cuts. Buses offer minimal connectivity on the islands and travel the majority of significant routes on the mainland. Renting a vehicle, scooter, or motorcycle is the best option to complement bus travel, particularly on the islands where rental outlets can be found in most major towns and resorts. Traveling between the islands entails using hydrofoils, catamarans, or ferries to reach any of the more than sixty inhabited isles. Internal flights can save literally days of travel time:

the trip from Athens to Rhodes takes two hours roundtrip, compared to 28 hours by boat. However, they are very expensive.

BY BUS.

Bus services on main routes run frequently, efficiently, and promptly at the designated times. The spacing between them is longer on secondary routes, yet even the most isolated communities are connected to the province capital every few days. When a boat arrives or departs an island, there are typically buses that connect the port and major town, if they are different. The nationwide network is managed by the KTEL (Kratikó Tamío Ellinikón Leoforíon; t14505 premium call charge and no national online timetable), a syndicate of commercial operators with a base in each county. Make sure you have the correct station for your departure because there may be multiple dispersed terminals for services in different directions in medium-sized or large towns.

On key departure points, computerized ticketing is available with allocated seating. On intercity routes like Athens–Pátra, these buses are frequently fully booked at the ekdhotíria (the office that issues tickets). On secondary rural/island lines, tickets are distributed on-the-spot by a conductor (ispráktoras), and seating is first come, first served with some standing permitted. There are no low-cost advance booking rates; the fare from Athens to Pátra is fixed at €27.

VIA TRAIN.

OSE (Organismós Sidherodhrómon Elládhos; t1110, wose.gr) manages the railway network on the Greek mainland; except in a few cases, trains are slower than comparable buses. Some lines are inherently pleasurable, none more so than the rack-and-pinion service between Dhiakoftó and Kalávryta in the Peloponnese, and they can be significantly cheaper - fifty percent less on non-express services (but nearly the same on express), even more if you buy a return ticket.

Timetables are supplied yearly in the form of compact booklets in Greek only; however, as services are being reduced as a result of ongoing austerity measures, it is preferable to check online, at station schedule boards, or at information counters. When you begin your journey at a station equipped with computerized amenities, you have the option to reserve a seat at no additional cost; your ticket will be printed with the carriage and seat number.

First and second are the two fundamental classes; the latter is roughly 25% less expensive. For departures between Alexandhroúpoli, Thessaloníki, Vólos, Kalambáka, and Athens, there is an express train category called Intercity (IC on timetables). When the line upgrade is finished, there will also be trains between Pátra and Kalamáta, though at the time of writing, all trains on that Peloponnesian route terminated at Kiáto, from where the journey is completed by bus transfers.

On the IC route between Athens and Thessaloníki, a second-class ticket costs €45 in person and €35 online, with sometimes-occurring special discounts as low as €9. A seat on the slower overnight train costs €25 (€19 online), while a sleeper costs €49 (€39 online).

Onboard tickets are subject to a fifty percent penalty; in contrast, non-express train tickets purchased during off-peak seasons are discounted by twenty-five percent for those under the age of twenty-six and sixty. Holders of passes for InterRail and Eurail must make reservations and pay express surcharges just like everyone else.

BY SEA.

Seagoing vessels come in a variety of forms: standard ferries, which never go faster than 17 knots; the new breed of "high-speed" boats (tahylóö) and catamarans, which typically transport cars and can reach speeds of up to 27 knots; roll-on-roll-off short-haul barges, also known as pandófles ("slippers"), hydrofoils, which are similarly swift but only carry passengers; and local kaïkia, which are small boats that go on short hops and excursions during certain seasons.

Ferry connections are shown in the "Arrival and Departure" sections of the book as well as on the route map. However, schedules are famously unpredictable and should be checked seasonally; information provided pertains to departures from late June to early September. There should be a minimum of two, perhaps three, daily departures available when sailing from Pireás to the Cyclades or Dodecanese throughout the sailing season. The number of departures during the off-season decreases significantly, with fewer inhabited islands connected only twice or three times per week.

At all island and mainland harbors of any size, the local port police (limenarhío) can provide trustworthy departure information; in the Athens area, there are offices at Pireás (t210 45 50 000), Rafína (t22940 28888), and Lávrio (t22920 25249). Automated phone answering services with an English option for scheduling information are available from busier port police. Many businesses publish yearly schedule booklets, but as the season progresses, they might not follow them. For up-to-date information, visit their websites, if any exist.

FERRIES

With a few subsidized outlying routes still operating with antiquated rust-buckets, the Greek ferry fleet is largely modern. Routes and speeds, however, might differ greatly; a trip from Pireás to Santoríni, for example, can take five to ten hours.

Unless you need to reserve a cabin berth or room for a car, it is advisable to purchase tickets the day before departure. Ferries must be reserved at least ten days in advance during peak travel times, such as Christmas/New Year's, the week before and after Easter, late July to early September, and the days surrounding election dates. You cannot purchase a ticket on board the majority of main lines because ticketing is done electronically. Even though a lot of firms let you book and pay online, tickets still need to be picked up at the dock at least fifteen minutes before the trip leaves.

If you don't say differently, you will be automatically sold the cheapest fare class, ikonomikí thési, which provides you access to the majority of boats with the exception of the upper-class restaurant and bar. The majority of more recent vessels appear to be specifically built to irritate summertime vacationers who try to sleep on deck. First-class double cabins with en-suite toilets can cost as much as a flight, while second-class cabins are usually quadruple; for long overnight travels, it's worth the few additional euros for a cabin bunk.

Separate tickets are provided for motorbikes and vehicles; depending on size, the cost of the latter has increased substantially recently to as much as five times the passenger fare. Sámos–Ikaría, for instance, costs about €12 per passenger or €40 per car, but Sámos–Pireás costs roughly €28/€100. Only larger islands such as Crete, Rhodes, Híos, Lésvos, Sámos, Corfu, or Kefaloniá are worth visiting by automobile, and then only if you plan to stay for a week or longer. If not, it will be less expensive to leave your car on the mainland and hire one when you get there.

Catamarans, hydrofoils, and fast boats.

Often referred to as "Flying Dolphins" or dhelfínia, hydrofoils are more than twice as costly as regular ferries; nonetheless, its network efficiently bridges gaps in ferry schedules, frequently offering more convenient departure times. Seasick people should avoid them even in mild seas, as they are the first ships to be canceled in inclement weather. This is their biggest disadvantage. Many cease operations or drastically cut back on how often they occur between October and June. It is not permitted for hydrofoils to transport bicycles or scooters.

Chaotically air-conditioned, catamarans and high-speed boats (tahþplia) typically lack deck seating and bombard you with Greek TV on numerous screens; upgrading to dhiakikriméni thési (upper class) just affords you a better view. Car fares are standard, however passenger tickets cost at least twice as much as a similar ferry ride, or around the same as hydrofoil rates. In the same way, a lot don't operate from October to April.

little boats.

During the season, tiny vessels called kaïkia and tiny ferries travel to some of the less well-known satellite islets as well as between nearby islands. Although they are frequently more enjoyable and very helpful than mainline services, they are rarely less expensive. The text mentions the more reliable kaïki linkages, but the quayside is where you may find solid information. Many islands are home to hordes of taxi boats, which transport passengers along prearranged routes to isolated beaches or ports that are difficult, if not impossible, to reach by land. These can come at a rather steep price, usually per person but sometimes per boat.

BY PLANE

Greek national carriers Olympic Airlines (including Olympic Aviation, t801 11 44 444, wwww.olympicairlines.com), Aegean Airlines (t801 11 20 000, wwww.aegeanair.com), and Sky Express (t281 02 23 500, wwww.skyexpress.gr) are in charge of scheduled domestic flights in Greece. Although the majority of their flights are to and from Athens or Thessaloníki, they cover a wide network of island

and mainland destinations. When it comes to pricing and service, Aegean frequently undercuts Olympic, even though its offerings are less frequent. Sky Express, which was founded in 2007, is expensive and limited to a few routes connecting Iráklio, Crete, with other islands. There aren't many walk-in town offices; instead, all three airlines focus mostly on online and call center e-ticket sales. Commission on tickets purchased through travel companies is charged at least €10.

The cost of fares to and from the islands is at least double that of a deck-class ferry ride; nevertheless, on inter-island routes that are poorly served by boats (such as Rhodes–Sámos), this time is well spent, and certain subsidized peripheral routes actually end up being less expensive than a hydrofoil or catamaran trip. Aegean's lowest web fares are non-refundable and non-changeable; however, with Olympic, you can amend your travel date up to 24 hours before to departure, subject to availability, without incurring any fees.

During high season, reservations for island flights should be made at least one month in advance if they are a crucial component of your itinerary. There are waiting lists, which are worthwhile joining because cancellations happen almost daily. Aegean and Sky Express fly larger, more reliable aircraft, but many Olympic trips use tiny prop planes that are unsuitable for flying in high winds or, depending on the airport, after dark. If you have recently arrived from abroad or bought your ticket anywhere other than Greece, you are permitted to bring the regular international luggage weight limitations (20–23 kg).

BY CAR, MOTORCYCLE AND TAXI

Driving through Greece's breathtaking beach and mountain beauty is definitely a pleasure. But keep in mind that it has one of the highest rates of fatal accidents in all of Europe. Local drivers frequently engage in horrible driving behaviors, such as cutting corners too quickly, pulling out of side streets without signaling, and overtaking on bends. Another significant problem is drunk driving, particularly late at night, on Sunday afternoons, and on public holidays.

Poor road conditions can include uneven pavement, insufficient signage, and unmarked railroad crossings. There are a few, but increasing, motorways with tolls (€2-3) that total up to over €30, like on the route from Athens to Thessaloníki, for instance. Currently, the price of fuel, be it diesel, super, or ordinary unleaded (amólyvdhi), is more than €1.65 per litre nationwide, and frequently exceeds €1.80 in some isolated regions. Be advised that a lot of gas stations close on Sundays and after 8 p.m., making it difficult to find one during such times in rural areas.

Due to oversubscription, parking is a problem in practically every town on the mainland as well as the largest island centers. Pay-and-display methods are prevalent, as are resident-only programs, and it's rarely obvious where tickets can be obtained.

Driving regulations

In Greece, as in continental Europe, you drive on the right. The first car to approach a one-lane bridge and vehicles going uphill both demand their right of way; in this case, flashing headlights indicate that the other motorist is adamant about passing or coming through. On the other hand, if someone is approaching you quickly and repeats this sign, it indicates that there is a police control point up ahead.

Children under the age of ten are not permitted to ride in the front seats of cars, and violators face fines. It is mandatory to use seat belts when riding a scooter or motorcycle. Driving away from an accident of any kind is prohibited, as is moving the cars before the authorities show up. If the other party has suffered significant injuries, you may be detained at a police station for up to 24 hours.

Rent a car

During high season, the cost of renting a car in Greece for the smallest car from a local chain or one-off store starts at about €300 per week, which includes unlimited mileage, insurance, and tax. At other times, you may get conditions of €30 per day, all inclusive, at smaller local outfits; if you book in advance online, you can get even better rates for stays of three days or longer. Open jeeps can be rented for between €65 and €100 per day.

Personal insurance and collision damage waiver (CDW) are hardly ever included in rental costs in Greece. The deductible charge for the CDW is usually between €400 and €600, and it can be applied to even the smallest scratch or missing mudguard. It is highly advised that you pay the additional €5-7 each day for full coverage in order to prevent this. Regular travelers might think about purchasing annual excess insurance from Insurance 4 Car Hire (www.insurance4carhire.com), which covers drivers based in the UK and North America.

The minimum age restrictions vary from 21 to 23 years old, and all agencies will request a blank credit card slip as a deposit (which is deleted when you return the vehicle securely). Any motorist in the European Economic Area may use a driving license from any member state; however, all other drivers (contrary to what certain dishonest agencies may say) need an International Driving Permit. If you are stopped by traffic authorities without an IDP, you could be charged and taken into custody.

Reliable Greek or smaller international chains with multiple locations include Avance, Antena, Auto Union, Payless, Kosmos, National/Alamo, Reliable, Tomaso, and Eurodollar; all are less expensive than Hertz, Sixt, or Avis. The book includes specific recommendations for the area.

Bringing your own vehicle

In the event that you plan to drive your own vehicle to and from Greece, keep in mind that insurance obtained in one EU member state is transferable to another, however this frequently only provides third-party coverage. Because of the fierce competition in the market, many UK insurers will provide comprehensive, pan-European coverage for no cost or at a minimal cost for a maximum of sixty days. The Greek equivalent, ELPA, provides free road assistance to members presenting proof of AA/RAC/AAA membership. ELPA operates breakdown services on several of the major islands; in an emergency, dial 10400.

EU nationals who bring their own vehicles are allowed to drive around the nation unhindered for six months, or until the expiration of their domestic road tax or insurance, whichever comes first. Keeping a vehicle in Greece longer requires additional documentation. Non-EU citizens will have their car registered in their passport; a carnet often permits you to keep a car in Greece for a maximum of six months without paying road taxes.

Rentals of motorbikes and scooters

Greek words mihanákia or papákia (little ducks) refer to little motor scooters with automatic transmissions that are useful for transportation on all but the steepest terrain. For €12–18 a day, you may rent them on a number of islands as well as in several well-known mainland resorts. You can negotiate lower rates during off-peak hours or for a longer rental duration. Most islands are mountainous, and only 80cc and larger models are powerful enough for two riders.

The prevalence of genuine motorbikes, or mihanés, with safer tires and manual gearboxes is lower than it should be. In many resorts, bikes 125cc and up can be rented for about €20 a day with the right licence. Quads are also becoming more and more popular; they are undoubtedly the most ridiculous-looking and unusable form of transportation ever created, and they are highly unsteady when turning. Make sure you have helmets on.

Reputable businesses need any engine above 80cc to have a complete motorcycle driving permit (Class B); Greek legislation really specifies "over 50cc." Usually, a deposit of your passport is required. A significant punishment is also imposed for not having the appropriate license on you; yet, some organizations still require this as security rather than a passport.

A lot of rental companies will give you a crash helmet (krános), which is frequently ill-fitting, and some may require you to sign a liability disclaimer if you refuse it. It is legally compulsory to wear a helmet, and refusal to do so carries a fine of €185. However, on some tiny islands, the rule is not strictly enforced, while on other islands, police roadblocks erratically issue tickets to both foreigners and locals.

Always check the brakes and electrics before leaving the bike; dealers frequently leave the front brakes far too loose in an admirable attempt to save you from riding over the handlebars. As a backup to the batteries, make sure there is a kickstart as well, as ignition switches frequently malfunction. On scooters and motorcycles, you usually have to return the equipment if you break down, however the better shops will come to you for free.

Taxi

If you obtain a trustworthy driver who turns on the meter and doesn't use any fancy equipment to rig the reading, Greek taxis are some of the least expensive in the Mediterranean. Within city or town bounds, when Tariff 1 is applicable, using the meter is required; in rural regions, or between midnight and five in the morning, Tariff 2 is in force. Certain islands have fixed routes with set prices that may only leave when they are completely filled. Otherwise, the meter starts at €0.85 across Greece, with a minimum fee of €1.75; the cost of each piece of luggage in the boot is €0.35. In addition, there are surcharges of €0.80 for exiting a harbor area and €2 for entering or leaving an airport (€3 for Athens). There is a €1.50 fee if you call for a cab on spec; the meter starts as soon as the vehicle pulls up to your location. Each category of additional costs needs to be listed on a card that is attached to the dashboard.

Approximately one week leading up to and following Orthodox Easter and Christmas, a gratuity known as filodhórima, or ten percent, is required.

By bicycle

Unless it's summer, cycling in Greece is not as difficult as you might think. This is especially true if you rent a mountain bike, which is now the norm and usually costs no more than €8 per day. But you do need steady nerves because Greek drivers are famously irresponsible to bicycles and the majority of the country's roadways are small with no bike lanes or verges.

provided you possess a bike, you should think about traveling with it by train or plane (you can bring it free provided it doesn't exceed your 20–23 kg international baggage allotment; however, you must make advance arrangements with the airline to prevent exorbitant fees upon check-in). After arriving in Greece, you can bring a bike on most ferries for free, ride in the guard's van on most trains for a modest cost, and store it in the bus luggage bays. Since specialty stores are few, bring any little spare components you may need.

GREECE TOP EXPERIENCES

Greece is a haven for foodies, wine connoisseurs, and more, and it is home to some of the most stunning ancient sites and islands in the world. Explore bustling cities, walk up towering mountains, and relax on immaculate beaches along stunning coasts where the Mediterranean sun shines. These are the top experiences to cross off your list because of the varied terrain it offers.

MUST-SEE FAVORITES PLACES

Nearly every attraction under the sun may be found in Greece. Greece's capital, Athens, is a treasure trove of delights, from the Roman Agora and the temple-topped Acropolis to the marketplaces, tavernas, and museums. To spare you time and research, guides will point you the must-sees and tell you about their histories. Other choices include treks to Cape Sounion, Meteora, and historical Delphi; foodies can also indulge in Greek cuisine; and cruises around the Saronic Islands on leisurely days. But tours of Greece include more ground than just the mainland and Athens. Greece's 227 inhabited islands, which offer sublime catamaran sails and excursions around sugar-cube villages, wineries, monasteries, and beaches, are like siren calls. Among them are the stunning islands of Santorini and Mykonos.

Discover the Acropolis, Acropolis Museum and Sounio Temple

On a full-day private trip, take in some of the most famous and must-see sights in Athens, starting with the Acropolis, one of the most significant ancient sites in the world. Take a leisurely stroll around the Acropolis Museum, which houses numerous significant archeological discoveries, and then relish a picturesque drive to Cape Sounion. It is home to the almost 200-foot-tall ancient Greek temple of Poseidon, which was constructed there in the fifth century BC.

Wine Tasting on Santorini

Enjoy a memorable wine-tasting trip that takes you through the best spots in Santorini. In addition to enjoying the island's renowned wines and delectable regional fare like mussels and sea urchin salad, you'll be able to witness many of its highlights, including a sunset that is sure to impress.

Santorini Sunset Catamaran Cruise

Any visitor to Santorini has to experience one of the island's renowned breathtaking sunsets. The perfect private tour is offered by an opulent catamaran cruise that sails around the caldera cliffs. It includes a freshly prepared supper and drinks, and it ends with a sunset from one of the best viewpoint spots, Ammoudi Bay, which is located just below Oia village.

Crete Wine and Music Tasting Tour

Experience the exquisite wines of Crete with a trip that allows you to sample six varieties produced from local grapes while listening to lovely music performed by your host musicians. You'll meet with a ceramist in the pottery hamlet of Margarites before to this private performance to gain more knowledge about the craft and possibly even create a piece of your own.

Sail Around Beautiful Milos

Incredible beaches varying from white and black to shell- and pebble-covered may be found on the island that gained notoriety as the location of the Venus de Milo statue discovery. The greatest way to experience Milos is to go sailing across the surrounding sea, which is beautifully colored in tones of blue and green. You will be able to swim in those alluring crystal-clear waters, explore caves, pause at secret spots, and take in a breathtaking sunset.

Tour Knossos on Crete to Discover the Palace Myths

Discover the myths surrounding the historic Palace of Knossos on an outdoor adventure with a unique family-friendly tour. As you explore historical sites, engage in interactive activities, and play games inspired by the book At the Palaces of Knossos by author and philosopher Nikos Kazantzakis, knowledgeable educators make sure that all members of the family have a great day.

Sea Kayaking on Santorini

On a half-day sea kayaking tour, explore Santorini's natural beauties, such as the caverns that turn blue when light hits the water and the well-known Red Beach, which is noted for its flaming volcanic sands. You'll be able to snorkel, enjoy the exhilaration of cliff jumping at White Beach, and paddle about historic Akrotiri.

Discover the World of Naxian Marble

You can take advantage of special trips that will introduce you to the Naxian Marble universe. Visit a marble quarry to discover more about the extraction process, the island's usage of marble throughout history, and other topics. Even better, you may take part in a marble workshop and learn how to make a marble piece of your own to take home.

Mountainous Apeiranthos

Discover the everlasting beauty of Apeiranthos, a mountainous village on Naxos, by taking a tour that takes you down its marble walkways that are dotted with stone houses. Since it was highlighted on Anthony Bourdain's "Parts Unknown," it has gained some notoriety as a culinary destination. In one of the traditional restaurants, you may try a variety of meals made using regional ingredients.

Take a Santorini cooking class.

Entire the culinary experience by enrolling in a cooking lesson in a typical Santorinian home, led by Petra Kouzina. After a quick introduction to the island's cuisine and specialties, you'll take home-style cooking classes. The nicest part is when you share and savor the food.

BECOME A MYKONIAN FOR A DAY.

Take a day trip to Mykonos and experience life as a true local. Get to know the animals by going to one of the farms on the island. Enjoy the outcomes of your participation in the bread baking, cheese manufacturing, and goat milking processes over breakfast, along with other locally produced items. Swimming on a secluded private beach and island exploration by 4X4 are also included in the excursion.

Take a Cooking Class with Mykonians and Visit the Sacred Site of Delos

When visiting Delos, a UNESCO-protected site housing some of the most extensive remnants of the golden age of classical Greece, taking a boat tour is a must. There are also excursions that allow you to explore the site and then participate in a Mykonian cooking class to sample the cuisine.

LITTLE VENICE AT SUNSET WITH DELOS AND RHENIA ISLAND IN THE BACKGROUND.

Discover the history of one of the most significant archeological sites in the nation, Delos, and then have a swim in the glistening blue seas off one of the immaculate beaches of Rhenia Island for an amazing experience. Savor a seafood pasta dinner paired with wine, then end the evening with a sunset viewed from Little Venice on Mykonos.

AN ALL-DAY TRIP FROM ATHENS TO HYDRA.

Hydra, which is less than two hours from Athens, is a perfect day trip destination where you'll feel as though you've traveled back in time. The peaceful cobblestone lanes are perfect for exploring on foot, by donkey, or on horseback. Savor traditional Greek cuisine at one of the seaside tavernas while swimming in the alluring blue waves.

After leaving Santorini, take a leisurely stroll and e-bike tour of Thirasia.

Don't pass up the opportunity to experience this enjoyable walking and electric mountain bike excursion on Thirasia Island, which is close to Santorini. Sometimes referred to as Santorini fifty years ago, you may ride through untamed, wild landscapes to the Monastery of Kimisis, where you can eat lunch and fresh-baked warm bread, among other things.

A Whole Day Wine Tour of Nafplio and Nemea.

Designed with wine connoisseurs in mind, a day tour via Nemea and Nafplio will introduce you to one of the nation's most significant wine-producing regions. See two wineries for tours and tastings after taking a picturesque drive through the vineyards known for producing Agiorgitiko wine, which has been farmed here for thousands of years. Included are landmark locations in Nafplio as well.

A Photo Tour of Magnificent Meteora.

Take a private guided tour to Meteora, one of the most breathtaking and revered sites in Greece, with local photographers. You may take pictures of the area's caverns, monasteries, and rock formations while learning about its history on an all-day photo tour. Many professional recommendations are included in the experience to guarantee that you acquire those amazing images.

Minoan Food and Art on Crete.

Join a trip to explore the island's gastronomy, wine, history, and culture for a truly memorable dining and artistic experience in Crete. Discover a range of activities, such as the historical tales of Malia Minoan Palace, a cooking class featuring a three-course meal served in a family-style setting, and a painting class inspired by the Minoan culture.

Go on a day trip to Athens and discover Ancient Delphi.

Take a day trip to the UNESCO-listed site of ancient Delphi and learn about the legendary oracle of ancient Greece. Admire historic landmarks and historical ruins, such as the Temple of Apollo and the Athenian Treasury, and then travel to a unique mountain community that is never visited by visitors, where traditional crafts and ancient rural customs are still carried out.

Sail to the Small Cyclades and Rina Cave by going around Naxos.

Sail from Naxos for an entire day and take in the stunning beaches and shoreline of the island as you make your way to Rina, one of the most stunning sea caverns with its surreal azure seas. After swimming or snorkeling in this breathtaking underwater environment, explore the Small Cyclades' Iraklia or Schinoussa.

Top Sights and Hidden Gems

This list of 11 hidden gems in Greece looks beyond popular sites, whether you're looking for a mountain getaway, a remote coastal resort, a secret harbor, or the site of a legendary war.

The nation has captivated tourists for millennia with its captivating mythology, captivating history, and breathtaking scenery. Beyond the grandeur of well-known tourist locations like Santorini and Athens, you can discover beauty and riches that could seem like your own private secrets.

Discover these undiscovered gems by embracing the beach charms of Kastellorizo or traveling back in time through the alleyways of medieval villages on the island of Chios.

Kastellorizo

Situated fewer than 2,625 feet from the Turkish coast, this charming island at the edge of the Dodecanese stubbornly defends its Greek identity.

The small island has served as a junction for major civilizations and nautical tribes for millennia. Zeus's birthplace offers panoramic views, Byzantine monasteries, and striking blue-and-white-sand Mediterranean contrasts.

You can experience a level of history and antiquity that few other locations can match by touring Kastellorizo. The secluded and idyllic village showcases Greece's history, spanning from the Neolithic era to the knights of St John and the 19th-century fishing legacy.

Highlights include the main town, Palaiokastro, Castello Rosso, cliff diving, and snorkeling.

It is advised to stay for two to three days.

Travelers can take a flight from Athens to Rhodes, where they can take a ferry to reach Kastellorizo on Rhodes.

Ithaca

The Odyssey, a Homeric legend, made reference to the beautiful island of Ithaca, which helped bring it to popularity thousands of years ago. The remote sandy beaches and charming fishing villages of the Ionian island have not lost their legendary charm.

The famous architecture shimmers against the fjord-like bay, while boutique hotels provide a touch of modern elegance. This island offers something different, with over thirty archaeological sites mixed up with vibrant eateries.

Without the throngs of Mykonos and other islands, Ithaca offers the colorful promenades and glitz of Greece's white sand beaches. If you decide to go to Ithaca, you can take romantic afternoon strolls on Greece tours for couples or enjoy the seaside vibe of Greece at sleepy, traditional tavernas or on isolated shores.

The highlights: Filiatro Beach, Gidaki Beach, Sarakiniko Beach, Kathara Monastery, and Paralía Fríkes

It is advised to stay for two to three days.

Traveling by air from Athens to Kefalonia and then ferry from Kefalonia to Ithaca is one way to travel to Ithaca.

Milos

The Aegean Sea's most spectacular scenery can be found in Milos. Its beaches contrast with the emerald hues of the lake, glowing pink and orange. The shoreline is also covered in rocks that resemble the moon, which can be examined from the glistening water.

Hidden caverns reveal stories of medieval pirates, and quaint houses sparkle with vivid hues. The limitless natural wonders, the archeology museum, and the old catacombs are perfect for families and couples to explore.

Luxurious resorts with expansive views of the seascape may be found on the summer island. When on tours or vacations in Milos, visitors can enjoy the serenity of these hotels, many of which are perched on the isolated hills that rise up to the beachfront.

The highlights: Sarakiniko Beach, Kleftiko Beach, Firiplaka Beach, Tsigrado Beach, and Milos Mining Museum

It is advised to stay for two to three days.

Traveling to Milos can be done by boat from Santorini, Mykonos, Paros, or Naxos, or by plane from Athens.

Paxi

Paxi's white-pebbled beaches and sapphire waters are overlooked by three quaint harbor settlements. Amidst lush vineyards, ancient olive groves ascend the hillsides inland. Between towns and pristine bays surrounded by towering limestone cliffs, taxi boats make their way.

The adjacent island of Antipaxi is home to opulent houses, wild myrtle, pine, and cypress trees, while the capital's highly appreciated Venetian architecture accentuates Paxi's unique beauty. On guided or self-directed tours, you may discover the rich history of the picturesque villages with sweeping views of the Ionian Sea.

Travelers can immerse themselves in the antiquity that seeps from the fantasy villages by the sea, or they can enjoy the cosmopolitan charms of vibrant Paxi. Those on luxury trips and vacations in Greece are invited to enjoy the peace and quiet on remote beaches or to explore the pristine waters on opulent yachts.

Highlights include Blue Caves, Gaios, Tripitos Arch, Vrika Beach, and Voutoumi Beach.

It is advised to stay for two to three days.

Travelers can take a flight from Athens to Corfu and then a ferry from Corfu to Paxi.

Chios

There are 24 intact medieval villages on the uncharted island of Chios. The remains of impenetrable strongholds, geometric designs, unique architecture, and the production of mastic offer insights into the island's civilization.

Each village's distinct design demonstrates the range of customs that exist in the area. Travelers can walk across rooftops as they pass by tightly packed white houses overlooking seashore roads.

There are beautiful black-pebble beaches for tanning, abandoned settlements with a serene atmosphere, and gastronomic gems offering distinctive Mediterranean cuisine. The greatest time to visit the Greek islands is in the summer, when the shipwrecks and sea caves of Chios may be seen through fantastic offshore scuba diving.

Particular highlights: Nea Moni Monastery, Pyrgi, Mavra Volia, Anavatos, and Vroulidia

It is advised to stay for two to three days.

Traveling to Chios from Athens can be accomplished by plane or ferry.

Mani

The stunning region of Mani, which stretches along the southern borders of the Peloponnese, is composed of snow-capped mountains, pristine bays, steep hillsides, and amazing medieval villages tucked away amid flourishing olive trees.

The mythical underworld entrance, stalactites, and stalagmites can all be found in the network of coastal caverns. With a Poseidon temple at the tip of Europe, Cape Tenaro captivates the attention of tourists. Due to its initial appearance in Homer's epic poem, the Iliad, this place is noteworthy.

The Mani peninsula offers activities fit for all kinds of adventures and serves as a gateway to Greece's natural history that has been maintained. You can have a truly unique Greek experience by deviating from the typical route and visiting the distinctive villages of Mani. This will enable you and your family to enjoy the top 8 Peloponnesian activities.

Diros Caves, Cape Tenaro, Kalamata, Kardamyli, and Limeni are the highlights.

It is advised to stay for two to three days.

Mani may be reached via private transportation from Athens.

EPIRUS

Greece's northern province of Epiros showcases the diversity of the country with its natural beauties, ranging from lush woods to reflected highland lakes, in contrast to its famous beaches and historical history.

The Cycladic architecture of Mykonos and the remnants of the Athenian Acropolis seem worlds apart from Epirus. Rather, tourists are awestruck by the animals and Venetian relics, which include wolves, brown bears, and raptors.

The deepest valley in Greece is located in Epirus; neighboring towns offer breathtaking views of this remarkable structure during visitor tours. Trekking over the captivating terrain of the area will reveal smaller, genuine mountain communities.

Highlights include the Acheron River, the Vikos Gorge, Dodona, Ioannina Kastro, and the Bridge of Arta. Recommended stay duration: 2-4 days

Traveling to Epirus can be accomplished via plane from Athens or by ferry from Corfu to the port of Igoumenitsa in Epirus.

MONEMVASIA

Monemvasia, a historic castle town on an island off the east coast of the Peloponnese, has the atmosphere of a dream come true. Cratched out of the sea rock, the medieval fortification rises up the foothill with residences, arched alleyways, and steps.

Cobblestone streets with 13th-century architecture and elements of Ottoman, Venetian, and Byzantine influence are reminiscent of the medieval era. After unwinding in Turkish baths, take in expansive views of the Mediterranean from Venetian villas.

One of the greatest places to visit in mainland Greece is Monemvasia, a wonderful undiscovered gem that provides a variety of unforgettable experiences. Visitors can spend a day exploring the massive Kastania Cave's passageways or sipping Malvasia wines, which are renowned for being matched with Shakespeare's plays.

Highlights include the following: Christos Elkomenos, Agia Sofia Church, Monemvasia Fortress, Our Lady of Hrisafittisa, and Ano Poli

It is advised to stay for two to three days.

The best way to reach to Monemvasia is by private transportation from Athens.

Skopelos

Nestled between Skiathos and Alonissos, in the stunning blue waters of the Aegean Sea, is the white-washed town of Skopelos with an ochre roof. The idyllic seaside location has serene promenades connecting little houses that ascend the verdant and gold hills.

Travelers' attention has been drawn to Skopelos since it is well-known for serving as the backdrop for the movie Mamma Mia. Despite this, much of Skopelos' many charms—one of the world's most beautiful filming settings for vacations—remain undiscovered. The isolated beaches offer fantastic swimming, the hillside villages provide breath-taking views of the Aegean, and water sports offer exhilarating ways to explore Greece's seas.

Skopelos's food scene is particularly welcoming, bringing visitors to the exquisite flavors of traditional Greek cuisine. Stuffed sea urchins, rice-served barnacles, and lobster with orzo pasta are a few of the amazing Skopelos specialties to sample.

Highlights include Panormos Beach, Kastani Beach, Agios Ioannis Church, and Agios Riginos Monastery in Skopelos Town.

It is advised to stay for two to three days.

The easiest way to travel to Skopelos is to take a ferry from Skiathos to Skopelos after flying from Athens to Skiathos.

AMORGOS

Few people have Amorgos, a magnificent island in the Cyclades, on their vacation itinerarys. This is surprising given the island's gorgeous white dunes, amazing caves, and picturesque bays, which make discovering this undiscovered gem a pleasure.

Old paths meander across the stony terrain, leading to vantage positions with views of the glistening azure ocean. Wandering around these historic settlements will reveal strands of cultural tradition to untangle and reflect the interesting history of the early Cycladic Era.

Amorgos' beaches feature sandy sections and coves with pebbles that make for excellent snorkeling. You can take a boat tour across the ocean to visit deserted bays, or you can come back to the island and explore the less-traveled paths through the rocky areas of Amorgos.

Particular highlights: Mouros Beach, Chora Village, Agia Anna Beach, Hozoviotissa Monastery, and Maltezi

Suggested duration of visit: one to two days

How to get there: From Rhodes, Mykonos, Santorini, or Athens, take a ferry to Amorgos.

METEORA

One of the most amazing places in Greece is the archeological site of Meteora. Built into and on the enormous rock formations and sandstone pillars that rise out of the surrounding terrain, the monastic region is home to preserved monasteries.

Meteora, which rises to the people like natural columns, is a breathtakingly cinematic destination for off-the-beaten-path trips of Greece. The exhibits and artifacts found in the Byzantine monasteries are historical treasures.

Tours of one of Greece's top tourist destinations, Meteora, unveil a spiritual and religious side to the nation that few other locations can match. Travelers can see Greece's monastic hidden gem in a breathtaking location as a serene aura permeates the area.

Particular highlights: The Natural History Museum, the Great Meteoron Monastery, the Varlaám Monastery, the Ayía Triáda Monastery, and the Áyios Nikólaos Anapafsás Monastery

It is advised to stay for two to three days.

There are two ways to get from Athens to Meteora: via rail or private transfer.

LOCAL CULTURE AND CUSTOMS

Greece is essentially a fully integrated European nation, with minimal difference in conduct and social mores from your home country. However, if you look a bit closer or visit less visited, isolated locations, you'll see that the Greek methods have mostly survived. It's easy to unintentionally offend someone, but it's also very easy to prevent doing so by adhering to a few basic guidelines and changing your status from tourist to xénos, which is a word that refers to both stranger and guest.

Greeks are generally quite gregarious and inquisitive, to the point that it may come across as invasive, especially to a reserved British person. Be prepared to have your personal space invaded and to be asked personal questions, even from brief acquaintances. However, you could also receive invitations to people's homes, frequently so that you can get to know a sizable extended family. If you receive such an invitation, you should bring a little present, generally flowers or cakes from the neighborhood cake shop, and you are not expected to come on time—a half hour late is normal. You can offer to pay for dinner if you're invited, but it's highly doubtful that you'll be permitted to do so, and pressing the issue too much might be seen as impolite.

Traditional festivities

Name day celebration

The majority of Greeks get their names from holy saints. One very significant custom is that on a specific day of the year, everyone whose name derives from a saint revered by the church celebrates that saint's name. Someone's friends and family pay him a surprise visit on his "name day" and give him tiny gifts and well wishes. The guests are served pastries, candies, and hors d'oeuvres by the hostess of the house. Name days hold greater significance in Greece than birthdays.

May Day

Greece's May Day (Protomagia) celebrations date back to the ancient customs honoring Demeter, the goddess of agriculture and harvest, which marked the unmistakable end of winter and the beginning of summer. These celebrations also honored the fertility of the fields and the earth's fruitfulness. These days, people make flower wreaths to hang on their doors as a sign of fertility and good fortune. In Greece, Labor Day events align with Protomagia.

Engagement

In Greece, it is customary to become engaged before getting married. While the two families bring gifts to the bride and groom, the guy must ask the woman's father and close relatives for her hand in marriage. Wedding rings are exchanged; each is worn on the left hand. These rings will be worn on the right hand following the wedding. In Greece, becoming engaged can take years, and it's considered a commitment to the families. While it is slowly vanishing, this ritual is still prevalent in the Greek islands and mainland.

Carnival

The Carnival is known as "Apokries" in Greece. The celebration lasts for two weeks, starting on the Sunday of Meat Fare and concluding on Clean Monday (Kathari Deutera), the first day of Lent. Parties are held in the streets and clubs, when people dress up and toss colorful confetti to one another. The city of Patra has the most well-known carnival parade. Local customs are being revived in numerous cities throughout Greece and the Greek islands. The origins of the Carnival are thought to lie in paganism, specifically in the ancient celebrations honoring Dionysus, the god of feasting and alcohol.

Clean Monday

Lent or Clean Monday Monday is Saracosti, the first day of Lent, when families picnic and fly kites in the countryside.

Easter

For Greeks, Easter is a much more significant holiday than Christmas. On Good Friday or Good Saturday, women prepare buns and color eggs crimson. The Epitaphios, or Christ's tomb with its flower-decorated icon, is removed from the church on Good Friday, the day of grief, and then slowly dragged around the hamlet. Following the procession's return to the church, Christians kiss the Christ picture.

On the eve of Holy Saturday, or Melalo Savato, everyone gets dressed up and heads to the church for a ritual. A candle from the Eternal Flame is lit by the priest, who then sings the psalm Christos Anesti, which means "Christ has risen," and offers the flame to the congregation to light their own candles. Just before midnight, all of the church's lights are turned off, signifying the silence and darkness of the tomb. One person to another passes the flame. People set off fireworks, and bells ring nonstop. After midnight, mayiritsa, tsoureki (Easter cake), and red eggs are served for the Good Saturday Dinner. The family grills the lamb on a spit on Easter Sunday.

Easter is most famously celebrated on the island of Corfu.

Greek Independence Day

The declaration of the Greek Independence War against the Ottomans on March 25, 1821, is celebrated on Greek Independence Day. This day is not only a national holiday but also a religious holiday honoring the Annunciation of the Virgin Mary.

The Ohi Day

Greeks commemorate October 28 as the day that, during World War II, Greek tyrant Metaxas forbade the Italians from invading their nation. On this day, which honors the valiant OXI (NO), most Greeks fly Greek flags from their windows and balconies, while the soldiers and schoolchildren march in a parade.

SUPERSTITIONS

Greek superstitions have their roots in either paganism or religion. They differ depending on the location.

THE EVIL EYE (MATI)

Some Greeks, particularly those living in rural areas, think that receiving jealous praise or jealous jealousy from another person can give someone the evil eye, or matiasma. When someone has the evil eye, they typically experience negative psychological and bodily effects. To free the individual experiencing agony from the negative effects of the evil eye in this situation, a xematiasma expert must recite a specific prayer. Those who believe in matiasma wear a charm, a small blue bead with an eye painted on it, to ward off the illness. In addition to being said to guard off bad luck, blue is thought to be the hue most likely to offer matiasma to those who have it.

SPITING

Spitting is thought to drive the devil and bad luck away. This explains why the others spit slightly three times, exclaiming "ftou, ftou, ftou," whenever someone breaks tragic news (accidents, deaths, etc.). Another instance is when someone praises an adult, child, or even newborn on their attractiveness; in order to prevent the recipient from giving him the evil eye, the complimenter must spit on the recipient three times (mati).

BLACK CAT

It is said that seeing a black cat will bring misfortune for the remainder of the day. It is also thought to bring misfortune for a period of seven years if a mirror or glass breaks.

HOBGOBLINS.

In Greek, the hobgoblins are called kallikantzari. Folk Christmas traditions describe the hobgoblins as short, ugly, and distorted beings. They dwell underground year-round and saw the tree of the year. They come up to the world and play several practical jokes on humans from Christmas till Epiphany Day

(January 6th). The local priest visits each home on Epiphany Day, dousing each room with holy water in an effort to drive the hobgoblins back underground.

Tuesday is the thirteenth.

In contrast to popular perception in the West, Tuesday the 13th, not Friday the 13th, is considered unlucky in Greece.

The phrase "Pisase Kokkino."

When two persons speak simultaneously, they must touch any red object within their near vicinity and pronounce the phrase "pise kokkino," which means "touch red." This occurs because Greeks consider saying the same thing to be auspicious and believe that if two people don't touch something red, they will fight or argue.

SPECIAL EXPERIENCES

Nearly every attraction under the sun may be found in Greece. Greece's capital, Athens, is a treasure trove of delights, from the Roman Agora and the temple-topped Acropolis to the marketplaces, tavernas, and museums. To spare you time and research, guides will point you the must-sees and tell you about their histories. Other choices include treks to Cape Sounion, Meteora, and historical Delphi; foodies can also indulge in Greek cuisine; and cruises around the Saronic Islands on leisurely days. But tours of Greece include more ground than just the mainland and Athens. Greece's 227 inhabited islands, which offer sublime catamaran sails and excursions around sugar-cube villages, wineries, monasteries, and beaches, are like siren calls. Among them are the stunning islands of Santorini and Mykonos.

SELF-GUIDED WALKING TOURS

There are some of the best hiking paths in Greece, which will entice you to come back for an even more fulfilling walking vacation as soon as possible. Greece offers a diverse range of hiking experiences for avid trekkers, encompassing breathtaking beaches, islands, and historic sites, as well as stone villages, rough peaks, and verdant gorges.

There is a wonderful walking trip for everyone, whether you wish to visit the stunning islands of Crete, Naxos, Santorini, or Andros; ascend Mount Olympus for breathtaking views; or travel deep into Greece to see the ancient treasures of Athens and Meteora.

You can discover Greece on a budget with these Greek walking tours, either self-guided or small-group.

CRETE SELF-GUIDED HIKE

Crete, the largest and most adaptable of the Greek islands, is abundant in natural beauty and full with remnants of its violent and ancient past. It combines wild, dramatic hills and breathtaking gorges with fishing communities that are only accessible by boat or foot, in addition to graceful Venetian ports.

Highlights of the Exploring Crete walking trip, which focuses on the western portion of the island, include the stunning Omalos plateau and the largest gorge in Europe, stretching 11 miles! This is a moderately paced, eight-day self-guided hike.

ZAGORIA SECRET VILLAGES WALKING TOUR

Greece is more than just its well-known islands; the traditional Zagoria Villages complex, located in the northwest of the country, spans an untouched, isolated area of the Pindos mountains, despite being poorly known to foreign tourists. Many of these ancient, stone-built settlements from the late 18th century are treasures of vernacular architecture and are located within what is now a designated conservation area. In a setting full of stunning wildness featuring towering peaks, deep chasms, and vast natural forests, lose yourself in the natural world. The Guinness Book of Records states that the Vikos Gorge is the world's deepest canyon (relative to its width), and traversing it is part of the Zagoria: Secret Villages excursion. Note that this is a self-guided, eight-day walk.

SANTORINI AND NAXOS ON FOOT SELF-GUIDED WALKING TOUR

Two of the most stunning Greek islands, Santorini and Naxos, are well-known for their vivid, whitewashed cube-shaped homes and provide lots of walking options. One of the main highlights of the journey is exploring two islands with dramatically different sceneries.

The largest island in the Cyclades, Naxos, is home to fertile valleys, immaculate sandy beaches, a bustling harbor, and the enormous marble doorway of Portara, a landmark that dates back more than 2,500 years. Santorini, on the other hand, is known for its postcard-perfect sunsets and the archaeological site of Akrotiri, the so-called "Greek Pompeii." The 8-day self-guided walking tour, Santorini and Naxos on Foot, is rated as beginner to moderate.

Andros Trail Self-Guided Walk

The European Ramblers Association has acknowledged Andros as the first island in Europe because of "Andros Routes," a sustainable tourism initiative that has been upholding and repairing an old system of hiking trails. On the mountainous island of Andros, the northernmost of the Cyclades archipelago, trails used to be the only means of transportation between villages long before motorized transport arrived.

The Andros Trail is a well-marked path where you may walk past masonry and monuments that attest to their historic legacy. In recent years, a group of dedicated volunteers went about revitalizing this old network of roads. Admire the expansive coastline, stop at pristine beaches, stroll through charming towns, and indulge in Greek food at neighborhood tavernas.

Mount Olympus Guided Walk

The nation's oldest national park, Mount Olympus, is the highest mountain in the nation and the fabled abode of the ancient Greek gods. Its lower flanks are protected as a World Biosphere Reserve, and the park is a panorama of powerful plateaus, ridges, and gorges. There are 52 peaks total, so expect breathtaking views as you go to them. Depending on the weather, you might even reach Mytikas, or the "nose," the highest peak on the mountain at 2,918 meters.

For those seeking a quick getaway in Greece, the 4-day Mount Olympus Guided Walk is ideal. This journey is escorted by a knowledgeable local guide.

Ancient Greece on Foot Holiday

A week of "live" Greek history classes that will enable you to cross off some of the most well-known must-see locations in the nation. After arriving in Athens, the "cradle of Western Civilization," you will visit the Oracle of Delphi and spend two nights beneath the nearly unreachable heights of Meteora.

Visiting the Acropolis Museum is one of the highlights of the Ancient Greece on Foot tour. The iconic museum, which opened its doors in 2009, is home to artifacts from the adjacent Acropolis of Athens archeological site.

Crete Mountains and Coast Guided Walk

The Crete Mountains and Coast Guided Walk will appeal to lovers of coastal landscapes, history, and traditional Greek culture. It is packed with highlights, including an ascent of Mount Gingilos (2080m), scenic walks through numerous gorges, including the longest in Europe, the Samaria Gorge, and sightings of the wild goats (Kri-kri) and griffon vultures on the Omalos plateau.

Even while walking is the main activity, there is plenty of time to bathe at pristine beaches, see coastal towns, and experience the warmth of specially chosen accommodations.

EXPLORING BARS AND LOCAL LIQUEURS

Greece is renowned across the globe for its delectable food, stunning scenery, and lengthy history. But one facet of Greek culture that is frequently disregarded is its drinking customs. Greek social life is heavily reliant on drinking, which is significant in many facets of Greek culture.

DRINKING IN GREECE

A COMMUNAL ACTIVITY OF THE GREEKS.

In the first place, drinking is a social activity in Greece. Greeks typically share their beverages with friends and family rather than having them by themselves. Greeks sometimes come together for long social gatherings over drinks at tavernas or cafes. These get-togethers frequently last for hours. Greeks very frequently spend whole afternoons or evenings drinking and mingling with others. For this reason, we recommend that you "hire" a table in Greece rather than just finding one!

GREEK LIQUEURS AND MEZE TO THE RESCUE

Many of the traditional spirits and cocktails found in Greece are essential to Greek social life and culture. These beverages, which include fruit-based liqueurs and spirits with anise flavors, are frequently savored with Greek food.

Greek spirits like ouzo, a transparent liquor with an anise flavor, are among the most well-known. Ouzedes, or tiny plates of food, are usually offered with ouzo when drinking in Greece. The beverage is intended to be sipped gently during a meal or social gathering. Apart from its taste of anise, ouzo also has a strong scent of licorice and a high alcohol level, usually 40% ABV.

Tipouro, another well-liked Greek liquor, is prepared similarly to ouzo but with grapes instead of anise. Usually sipped as an aperitif or digestif, tsipouro is frequently served with small plates of food, such as cheese, cured meats, or olives. Both clear and aged tsipouro are available; the aged type typically has a more nuanced and smoother flavor.

Similar to tsipouro, raki is another traditional Greek alcohol that is usually prepared with the leftover grape pressings from wine manufacture. Raki is usually served with mezedes or other small plates of food and is best enjoyed in the company of friends. Another classic Greek drink is calledrakomelo, which is created by mixing raki with honey and spices like cloves and cinnamon. If you're going out to drink in Greece during the winter, this is a popular cocktail that is frequently served warm.

Greece has a reputation for producing fruit-based liqueurs in addition to wine and traditional spirits. Usually created with a blend of fruits and herbs, these liqueurs are used as digestifs or after dinner cocktails. In Greece, quince, apricot, and cherry liqueurs are a few of the widely consumed fruit-based liqueurs.

These are but a handful of the several Greek distillates that are consumed throughout Greece. Greek distillates are an essential component of Greek culture and a must-try for tourists to Greece.

Greek cocktails

Greek cocktails combine classic Greek ingredients and spirits with contemporary mixology methods and tastes. When you go out to drink in Greece, you might wish to try these well-known Greek cocktails:

Greek liqueur Mastiha is traditionally prepared from the resin of the Mastiha tree. This makes Mastiha Sour. In a shaker, combine egg white, sugar syrup, lemon juice, and Mastiha liqueur to create a Mastiha Sour. Give it a good shake, strain it into a glass, and add a fresh thyme sprig as a garnish.

Metaxa Lemonade: Greek brandy Metaxa is frequently used as a mixer in mixed drinks. In a large glass with ice, combine Metaxa, lemon juice, sugar syrup, and soda water to create a Metaxa Lemonade. Mix thoroughly and add a lemon slice as a garnish.

Ouzo is a traditional Greek anise-flavored alcohol that is typically served with meze platters. This is the watermelon Ouzo Cooler. Muddle some fresh watermelon in a shaker with sugar syrup, lime juice, and ouzo to make a Watermelon Ouzo Cooler. Give it a good shake, strain into an ice-filled glass, and then pour soda water on top. Add a sprig of fresh mint as a garnish.

Greek Island Iced Tea: This concoction takes the traditional Long Island Iced Tea and gives it a Greek flavor. In a shaker, combine equal parts ouzo, Metaxa, tequila, gin, and lemon juice to create a Greek Island Iced Tea. Give it a good shake, strain into an ice-filled glass, and pour cola on top. Add a slice of lemon as a garnish.

Tsipouro Lemonade: As previously mentioned, tsipouro is a classic Greek grape-based drink that is frequently served as an aperitif. In a large glass with ice, combine tsipouro, lemon juice, sugar syrup, and soda water to produce a Tsipouro Lemonade. Mix thoroughly and add a lemon slice and a fresh rosemary sprig as garnish.

Greek wine

You should be aware of the following regarding Greek wine:

Greece is home to a wide variety of wine regions, each distinguished by its own distinct terroir and grape varietals. Greece's most well-known wine regions are Naoussa, Nemea, and Santorini.

Grape types: There are numerous native grape types in Greece, some of which are unique to the globe. Greek grape varietals such Assyrtiko, Agiorgitiko, Xinomavro, and Moschofilero are among the most well-liked ones.

Natural winemaking methods, such fermenting wine in clay amphorae or maturing wine in wood barrels, are a long-standing practice among Greek winemakers. Additionally, a large number of Greek wineries utilize biodynamic and organic farming.

Greek wine is produced in a variety of styles, such as dry whites, reds, rosés, and sweet dessert wines. Greek wines that are highly recognized include Naoussa Xinomavro, Nemea Agiorgitiko, and Santorini Assyrtiko.

Food Pairings: In Greece, drinking is almost always accompanied by food! Fresh ingredients and robust flavors characterize traditional Greek food, which is frequently paired with Greek wine. Greek wine is often paired with grilled meats, feta cheese, and fresh seafood.

All in all, Greek wine is a distinctive and fascinating subset of wine that is well worth discovering. Greek wine delivers an authentic flavor of Greece's rich cultural heritage and terroir thanks to its rich history, distinctive grape varietals, and natural winemaking practices.

Getting Around Sensibly: Greek Beer and You

Naturally, a talk about Greek drinking customs would not be complete if it did not touch on the significance of moderation in intake. Greeks take great pleasure in knowing when to say when, even if they are known for their love of wine and spirits. Through moderation in the consumption of alcoholic beverages and observance of regional laws and customs, tourists can thoroughly experience the diverse and vibrant Greek drinking culture without going overboard.

To sum up, drinking like a Greek means appreciating the sense of hospitality and companionship that goes along with the beverage's flavor. Raise your glass, enjoy every taste, and raise a glass to Greece's ageless customs and rich culture.

AVOIDING TOURIST TRAPS

Greece and its stunning islands welcome millions of visitors each year who come to enjoy endless sunshine, warm blue waters, authentic Greek cuisine, and charming whitewashed towns and villages. But as with other well-known locations across the globe, there are tourist traps.

Tourist traps in Greece can waste your time and money, whether it's an unauthentic souvenir shop, an overpriced photo location, or locals trying to charge you more than they should.

We've made the decision to assist because there are a lot of things you should avoid doing while there if you want to have an authentic experience. Check out these tourist traps in the Greek islands to discover more.

Exploring the Most Well-liked Islands

A simple strategy to steer clear of tourist traps in the Greek islands is to go to the less well-known islands, where costs are typically lower and the population is less. While stunning locations like as Santorini and Mykonos are available, it can be challenging to avoid tourist traps.

There are expensive hotels, souvenir shops, upscale dining options, and sizable crowds near well-known beaches and attractions. Visit a more serene location to get a more genuine experience.

Folegandros is a prime example. Though it shares many amenities with Santorini, this lovely island is far more tranquil, inexpensive, and laid back. Keeping this in mind, resist the temptation to click on Instagram-worthy travel spots.

Dining on the Beach

Eating in the cafes, restaurants, and bars that line the beaches is one of the main tourist traps in Greece. In order to attract vacationing tourists, food costs at beachside establishments are nearly always inflated. Food made in a taverna a few streets back can often be 20% to 30% less expensive than food ordered at the beach.

Eating before or after your beach excursion is the best way to avoid falling victim to this tourist trap. Alternatively, bring a little snack so you may eat it when you get there. In any case, if you want to save money and maintain the integrity of your budget, avoid dining on the beach.

TRAVELING AROUND BY TOUR BUS

Tour buses provide a practical means of seeing the key sights of an island in a condensed length of time. Tour busses, on the other hand, are typically more costly than local transportation and arrive at an overpriced tourist shop in a remote location. Traveling across the islands by native transportation is a more genuine experience.

You'll meet new people, discover hidden gems that other tourists miss, and experience local life even though local transportation may take longer. Alternatively, instead of shelling out a lot of money for a bus tour, you might want to consider hiring a local tour guide for the day.

You'll be shown the greatest neighborhood eateries, brought to more authentic sites, and given greater insight into the island by someone who has spent the majority of their life there.

PURCHASING EXPENSIVE SOUVENIRS

While it's true that we all enjoy purchasing mementos to give to our loved ones back home from our trips, we don't have to spend excessive amounts of money on ostentatious and, to be honest, subpar items. In busy towns and at popular attractions, souvenir shops typically charge exorbitant prices for low-quality trinkets that, to be honest, no one wants to take home.

Thus, purchase something more modest and significant to save money and cheer someone back home. Sending home a postcard showing the locations you've been, for instance, has greater significance than an expensive, shoddy keychain. You might also bring some traditional Greek pastries or booze home with you, if space permits in your suitcase. In any case, this is preferable to squandering cash on mass-produced trinkets.

UTILIZING SOCIAL MEDIA TO VISIT RESTAURANTS

Spend a lot of money if you want to locate globally recognized restaurants that influencers frequent and feature on your Instagram page. Restaurants that have become virally popular are typically more expensive than equally good but lesser-known eateries.

Choose to eat at a neighborhood market or stop by a family-run taverna for a more genuine and affordable experience. These locations are generally calmer, allowing you to savor your meal in solitude, and they provide a more authentic Greek island experience at a more affordable price.

Purchasing Rooftop Views from a Chain Hotel

Just like you shouldn't go to restaurants that you only see on social media, you shouldn't book a meal at a chain hotel just because it offers a rooftop view. Travelers are now known on social media to visit opulent hotels purely to snap pictures from the restaurants and bars on the rooftops.

You'll spend more for these hotels, even though they provide an amazing experience. Drinks and food will probably cost more, in addition to the increased cost of your accommodation! This is made worse by the ease with which you may enjoy breathtaking views of the islands. You may take in classic views without having to deal with the viral rooftops, whether it's from a little neighborhood taverna or a neighboring overlook!

Purchasing Fake Designer Items

You can frequently find markets offering what seem to be the newest designer items at costs below market value on well-known Greek islands. Even while it sounds wonderful to score a deal, you should stay away from these stands because the products they are selling are probably phony.

Although most places fall victim to this tourist trap, it's still wise to be aware of it if you come across any phony designer goods. At a market, there are phony designer clothing goods, jewelry, and purses. The maxim "If anything seems too good to be true, then it probably isn't" is the greatest method to avoid falling into this trap.

Taking Sunset Photos on Santorini

You have probably seen the iconic sunset photos of Santorini with its vibrant, whitewashed houses and blue rooftops if you use Instagram. If you haven't, you've been living under a rock because this famous Greek island's picture has come to represent Greek island getaways.

Despite how calm this place appears to be, the reality is quite the reverse. There are long lines at dusk to snap a single picture of the white Anastasis Church with the flaming skies in the background. To ride the Santorini cable car, you may have to wait up to two hours. In light of this, if you wish to escape the throng around sunset, think about going somewhere else.

VISITING A RESORT THAT IS ALL-INCLUSIVE

Having fun at an all-inclusive resort is a possibility. You'll be close to everything you need, including food, drink, activities, and a swimming pool, to make the most of your stay in Greece. But part of the issue with all-inclusive resorts is that.

It is very tempting to spend all your time at the resort because everything is conveniently located there, but doing so would keep you from seeing the real Greece. Beyond the resort's boundaries lies a Greek paradise teeming with real food, friendly locals, globally recognized sites, and unforgettable experiences. Spend time away from an all-inclusive resort or avoid vacationing there if you want to enjoy all of this and more. Don't dine at your resort for every meal, for instance. Instead, go out to dine somewhere nearby.

NOT VERIFYING PRICES AT A RESTAURANT BEFORE EATING

Regretfully, overcharging tourists for food and drink at restaurants is a prevalent fraud on the Greek islands. Thus, it's imperative that you thoroughly peruse the menu and verify the costs prior to placing any orders at a restaurant. Avoid eating at a restaurant if it lacks a pricing list on its menu and won't tell you how much the food costs!

It's also important to look for any hidden trickery when perusing the menu. For instance, some restaurants charge for a cocktail as a shot, but each cocktail actually contains three or four shots, so the total may be three or four times higher when you go to pay. Do your homework and steer clear of this tourist trap as it has the potential to swiftly destroy your Greek island holiday.

GOING TO THE BIG ATTRACTIONS AT MIDDAY

In order to get up close to some of the most well-known monuments and landmarks, you'll have to navigate through crowds if you visit the Greek Islands during the busiest time of year. This not only ruins the real holiday experience, but it also takes up a lot of time.

Visiting before the throng gather in the morning is a great way to avoid this. You may be the only one at an attraction when everyone else is just getting out of bed if you get there right when it opens. Even better, it won't be that hot yet, making you feel more at ease and at ease while you go around.

THE TAXI TRAP

Make sure you inquire "how much" as you get into a cab—that is, how much roughly the fare will be to your destination—because cab drivers charge different amounts for passengers who don't ask.

ACCOMMODATIONS AND DINING

The Greek Islands are always in style, but being one of the most popular summer vacation spots worldwide, they truly came back to prominence last season. You're in for a treat if it has been a while since you've gotten a little taste of island life. World-class resorts and boutique hideaways are among the new accommodations that are prepared to greet visitors with open arms, breathtaking views of the ocean, and the finest seafood. While some are adult-only retreats perfect for a delayed honeymoon, others are family-friendly accommodations with roomy suites and engaging kids' programs. There are many of options, regardless of your preference.

BEST CULINARY EXPERIENCES IN GREECE'S TOP HOTEL RESTAURANTS

While lodging in Greece's best hotels, savor the country's vivid flavors and distinctive culinary customs. With the most mouthwatering culinary experiences, these guides will introduce you to the most opulent hotel restaurants and eating establishments.

Mavro Restaurant at Kivotos Santorini

With the best local ingredients and Mediterranean-inspired cuisine made by renowned chef Dimitris Katrivesis, Mavro Restaurant is a gourmet fantasy. With its opulent setting and stunning views of the Caldera, the restaurant provides a wonderful dining experience. Mavro Restaurant, tucked away in the center of Imerovigli, has grown to be a must-visit location for foodies and tourists looking for a unique taste of Santorini's culinary heritage.

The menu explodes with flavors that flawlessly blend the tastes of Santorini with the Chef's global travels, with a concentration on fresh fish, which is provided daily by local fishermen from the island's seaside towns. A delectable assortment of meals showcasing this renowned chef's culinary prowess will be served to guests.

Botrini Mykonos

The newest eatery of the renowned Katikies Group, Botrini's Mykonos, has just recently opened. Hector Botrini introduces his culinary wizardry to the opulent Katikies Mykontheos hotel, following the enormous success of Botrini's Santorini, the first Cycladic iteration of the renowned and Michelin-starred Athens restaurant housed at Katikies Santorini. Serving as the head chef of all hotel restaurants, Botrini crafts delectable dishes that captivate the palates of all guests. Situated above Agios Ioannis's sunny beach, Botrini's Mykonos presents a breathtaking Cycladic scene with a backdrop of the azure Aegean Sea and a unique, bohemian-chic vibe. Modern cuisine produced with fresh, seasonal ingredients from around the world, such as pasta, seafood, and beef, are offered on the menu. The restaurant pledges to transform Mykonos' culinary scene while staying true to the principles that have brought Botrini multiple accolades and a Michelin star.

Matsuhisa in Paros

The much-awaited debut of a new Matsuhisa restaurant in the center of the Cyclades on the island of Paros has recently delighted the Greek culinary scene. The new restaurant, which promises to redefine Cycladic hospitality with its unmatched degree of grandeur and sophistication, is the ideal fit for the opulent 5-star Avant Mar hotel, owned by Grivalia Hospitality. The new Matsuhisa restaurant is the major attraction, accompanied by a variety of excellent services like a store, traditional pastry shop, spa rooms, and an outdoor theater. Famous chef Nobu Matsuhisa has introduced his signature food to

Paros, bringing his culinary talents to the island. Matsuhisa's Nobu-style cuisine, which blends Peruvian and Japanese ingredients, serves guests exquisite and genuine dishes while they enjoy breathtaking views of the Aegean.

GALAZIA HYTRA RESTAURANT, SUMMER SENSES * PAROS

Greek food, with its strong regional flavor and seasonality, and the welcoming wine list make the ideal combination for a truly dreamy vacation to the charming town of Paros and Summer Senses Resort. Hit the ground running with a meal at the well-known Galazia Hytra restaurant, which has taken over Paros and the Cyclades after imitating its Michelin®-starred equivalent Hytra in Athens. A top-notch menu that dazzles with its exquisite simplicity is composed of imaginative takes on traditional Greek recipes and flawless ingredients. The stunning views of the charming Piso Livadi harbor and the lights of Naxos island enhance the trip even further.

THE COAST BY TAMARISK AT NUMO IN CRETE

Savor a fine dining experience in a romantic setting with stunning views of the sea at The Coast by Tamarisk, where food is enjoyed in a whole new way. Tucked away among tamarisk trees, this hidden treasure of a restaurant offers a private setting with tables that nearly touch the ocean. With carefully chosen premium ingredients like creamy mashed cauliflower, drizzled with cilantro oil, and delicious scallops with garlic butter, each meal is expertly cooked. For the discriminating palate, the ponzu-marinated oysters are yet another exquisite treat.

PERE UBU AT KALESMA MYKONOS

Since its opening in 2021, Kalesma Mykonos has become a beloved destination on the island due to its elegant decor and distinct ambience. The proprietors of the well-known Pere Ubu restaurant in Athens are the ones who created Kalesma, a contemporary destination restaurant with an emphasis on soul cuisine. The cuisine at Pere Ubu Mykonos, under the direction of chef Kostas Tsigas, is a highlight of the island's culinary scene. The cuisine is composed of aromatized organic ingredients, locally sourced goods, and fresh raw materials. Meanwhile, the fantastic sunset parties hosted by Zucca Radio's producers are complemented by elegant wine labels and delightful drinks for evening enjoyment. Special summer evening events, such barbeque nights, are also hosted at the hotel.

Barbouni Restaurant at Costa Navarino

In the center of Messinia, Barbouni Restaurant provides a distinctive dining experience at the stunning Costa Navarino resort. Fresh seafood and classic Greek cuisine are the restaurant's main specialties, with an emphasis on using seasonal and local ingredients. Eat outside on the terrace with breathtaking views of the Mediterranean Sea, and you'll be pampered with delectable cuisine and friendly service in a lovely environment.

Olvo at MINOIS Hotel in Paros

Experience the culinary symphony at "Olvo," where every dish has a distinct personality and fiery temperament. The gastronomic experience that Chef Alexandros Tsiotinis and his exceptional crew have created celebrates the earth's richness and the ever-changing bounty of seasonal foods. Every time a client visits "Olvo," they are in for a singular and wonderful experience that celebrates local produce and culinary customs.

Milos at Xenodocheio Milos in Athens

Founded by Costas Spiliadis, the first Milos hotel in the world has opened in Athens. It features a restaurant that adheres to the brand's minimal interference and respect for the finest quality materials and products in cooking. Taste the Mediterranean delicacies of Greece at xenodocheio Milos and take in the opulent surroundings of the hotel.

Santa Marina, a Luxury Collection Resort, Mykonos

In addition to a choice of 13 expansive villas, a beach club set in a cove protected from the strong Cycladic winds, and two infinity pools to vary the panorama while relaxing, Santa Marina has 101 Seaview rooms and suites with private plunge pools. The inventive plates served at two restaurants, Buddha-Bar Beach Mykonos and Mykonos Social by Jason Atherton, include Asian-inspired poke and ceviches inspired by the abundance of fish in the Mediterranean, as well as taverna-style dishes like slow-cooked lamb, sun-dried grilled octopus, classic horiatiki, and bread baskets accompanied by traditional dips like taramosalata (roe puree) and htipiti (spicy whipped feta).

USEFUL PHRASES AND WORDS TO LEARN

You intend to travel to Greece, then. Choosing which sandals to carry and locating the cheapest airfare may be your main priorities. But remember to learn a few Greek words before you leave to tour the breathtaking ruins and whitewashed towns of the nation. Although there are many useful tools available, such as computerized translators, mastering the fundamentals of a language is always polite.

Although nearly everyone in many tourist destinations knows basic English, learning a few popular phrases (and even a little Greek slang) will help you get the most out of your trip. You'll know you made an effort when locals give you a free slice of baklava or an ouzo shot after your dinner.

The translations that are written in Greek initially are listed below. The phonetic pronunciation is given in parenthesis, with the capital letters designating the stressed syllables. Try using Google Translate to hear an audio version of these sentences or downloading a language learning app.

Nobody wants to assume that everyone knows English when traveling overseas and become an annoyance. You should have no trouble speaking enough Greek to get by as a considerate tourist with a few pointers and some practice.

BASIC GREEK WORDS AND PHRASES

Hello: Γειά σου (YAH-soo)

The less formal way to say "hi" would just be Γεια (yah). If addressing a group, say Γεια σας (YAH-sas).

Nice to meet you: Χάρηκα πολύ (HA-ree-ka po-LEE)

How are you?: Τι κανείς? (tee-KAH-nis)

Good morning: Καλημέρα (kah-lee-MER-ah)

This greeting is valid until midday, after which Γεια(yah) is the customary greeting for the remainder of the day.

Good afternoon/evening: Καλησπέρα (kah-lee-SPER-ah)

When it's becoming late in the afternoon or evening, use this greeting.

Goodnight: Καληνύχτα (kah-lee-NEEKH-tah)

Say this when going to bed.

Thank you: Ευχαριστώ (eff-kha-ri-STOE)

Keep in mind that a courteous traveler is a good tourist.

Please/You're welcome: Παρακαλώ (para-kah-LOE)

Since "please" and "you're welcome" are the same word in Greek, learning how to pronounce them is simple. Saying Παρἱκἱλώ (para-kah-LOE) is appropriate when requesting directions or the cost of anything. It can also signify "huh?" or "I beg your pardon?" when you want someone to repeat something or when you've misunderstood something.

My name is...: Με λένε... (may LEH-neh)

What is your name?: πως σε λένε? (pos-oh LEH-neh)

Goodbye: Γειά σου (YAH-soo)

The informal way of saying bye would be Γεια (yah). Remember that this is equivalent to saying "hey" (aloha in Hawaiian or ciao in Italian). When speaking to a group, always remember to utilize the plural, Γεια σας (YAH-sas).

See/Talk to you later: Τα λέμε (tah-LEH-meh)

You might also hear folks using this phrase to wrap up a conversation.

Yes: Ναί (neh); No: όχι (OH-hee)

Take caution not to mix up yes and no. In Greek, όχι (oh-hee) is considered "okay," whereas ναί (neh) is incorrectly associated with "no" in English. The fact that they are the opposite of what you would first assume makes them simple to remember.

Excuse me/Sorry: Συγνώμη (See-GHNO-mee)

Say this to draw someone's attention, request permission to walk past, or express regret if you've accidentally run into someone.

I love Greece: Αγαπώ την Ελλάδα (Ah-gah-POH teen Eh-LAH-tha)

Oops! Ώπα! (OH-pa)

"Opa" is probably the one Greek word you are most familiar with. Originally meaning "oops" or "whoops," it is also commonly used to express joy and enthusiasm for food, dance, music, and beverages. Say "Opa!" in appreciation if your server offers you a round of ouzo shots on the house after you've thoroughly impressed him with your newly acquired Greek.

Greek Slang and Phrases

What's up/How's it going? Τι λέει? (tee-LEI)

What are you up to? Που είσαι? (pou-eeSAY)

So good/so cool: και γαμώ (kay-gaMOU)

Another option is to use μαλάκα (maLAka), which is a swear word in official usage. Everyone will use it informally to refer to friends; however, you should only use it with someone you know.

See you later: τα λέμε (ta LEH-meh)

Dude/man: ρε φίλε (reh-FEEleh)

CONCLUSION

In summary, Greece is a popular travel destination because of its captivating combination of rich historical and cultural heritage, breathtaking natural landscapes, and a wide variety of culinary delights. First-time visitors to Greece may find it challenging to adapt to or understand some Greek customs, habits, and practices.

It is not without difficulties, though, such as lodging, transportation, managing specific cultural customs, and safety issues.

Despite these obstacles, Greece is a must-visit for anyone looking for a combination of adventure, history, and relaxation because of the breathtaking beauty, one-of-a-kind experiences, and the friendly Greek people.

For this reason, before you travel to Greece and the Greek islands, we have compiled an extensive list of things you should know or keep in mind.

This book will help you better plan your trips, steer clear of unpleasant surprises, and become acquainted with Greek reality.

Printed in Great Britain
by Amazon